Antique Needlework

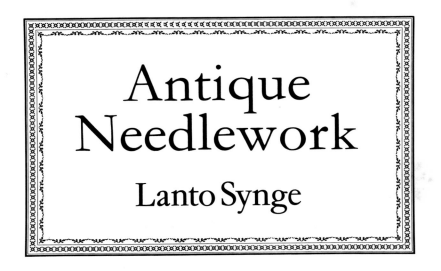

Antique
Needlework

Lanto Synge

BLANDFORD PRESS

POOLE   DORSET

First published in the U.K. 1982 by Blandford Press
Link House, West Street, Poole, Dorset, BH15 1LL

Copyright © 1982 Blandford Books Ltd

Distributed in the United States by
Sterling Publishing Co., Inc.,
2 Park Avenue, New York, N.Y. 10016.

British Library Cataloguing in Publication Data

Synge, Lanto
  Antique needlework.
  1. Needlework — History
  I. Title
  746.4   TT705

ISBN 0 7137 1007 1

Phototypeset by Oliver Burridge and Co. Ltd, Crawley, Sussex.

Printed in Singapore by Toppan Printing Co. (S) Pte. Ltd.

End Papers
Part of a large 17th-century bed cover,
perhaps Portuguese.

Plate 1 — Frontispiece
Part of a large tent stitch
hanging depicting Chinese
or Delft blue and white
vase filled with a variety
of flowers. English,
*c.*1740.

Opposite
Pair of canvaswork bell
pulls, *c.*1840.

Contents

Acknowledgements

I AM ENORMOUSLY GRATEFUL to many people for kindness and help. Mr Francis Egerton especially has spurred my enthusiasm with his great knowledge and boundless energy, and so many owners, curators, needleworkers and others in both Great Britain and the United States have given me much time and invaluable advice. I am greatly indebted to many authors of books and articles; my sincere thanks for their stimulation is recorded in the bibliography at the end of this volume. My sister-in-law, Mrs Teran Synge, repeatedly typed and altered the text with speed and efficiency.

I also wish to thank Mallett and Son (Antiques) Ltd for providing photographs, many by Jan Kot and Clive Bartlett. Dr Douglas Goodhart has kindly allowed me to reproduce several of his splendid early samplers. In addition the following have generously loaned photographs, or allowed pieces to be photographed: Le Curé de Saint-Bertrand-de-Comminges; His Grace the Duke of Buccleuch and Queensberry, K.T.; Sir John Carew Pole, Bart, D.S.O., T.D.; Hubert Chesshyre Esq., Chester Herald; Christie's; Christie's South Kensington; The Vicar and Church Wardens, Cogenhoe; Connecticut Historical Society; Beryl Dean; Francis Egerton Esq.; Mrs Audrey Field; Christopher Gibbs Ltd.; Michael Gillingham Esq.; Mrs Cora Ginsburg, Ginsburg and Levy; Hierloom and Howard Ltd; James II Galleries; Jeremy Ltd; Mayorcas Ltd; Moolham Mill Antiques; Musée Historique des Tissus, Lyons; The National Trust; Anthony Scaramanger Antiques; Sotheby's; Sotheby's Belgravia; The Vicar and Church Wardens, Steeple Aston; L. G. Stopford Sackville Esq.; The Master and Fellows of Trinity College, Cambridge; David Seton Wills Esq.

The Overlord Embroidery, part of which is illustrated, is displayed in the Overlord Gallery, at Whitbread in Chiswell Street, London EC1.

Plate 26 is reproduced by gracious permission of Her Majesty the Queen.

In addition I am particularly grateful to Mr John Chesshyre, Marlene Davis-Goff, Victor Frances Gallery, Hotspur Ltd, Mr Peter Maitland, Miss Jane Stevens and Lady Victoria Wemyss for valuable guidance, and to Miss Felicity Carter at Blandford Press for her help and great patience.

For my mother and father

The invisible things of Him since the creation of the world are clearly seen, being perceived through the things which are made, even His everlasting power and divinity.

Introduction

Pray, sir, take the laudable mystery of embroidery into
your serious consideration

THE HISTORY of needlework is intriguing and diverse, with a world-wide richness and broad, human implications. A study of it takes us into many periods of social history, since embroidery is one of man's oldest skills, referring us to each branch of the fine and decorative arts and pointing to fascinating interplays of influence and inspiration. The ancientness of the art has given it a unique depth while the simple occupation of making patterns and images with needle and thread has been the humble basis for the creation of many objects of great beauty.

We are fortunate to be living at a time when, as students or collectors, we have easy access to a vast range of material and can consult people with wide or specialised areas of knowledge. We can visit many great collections in public and private ownership, while the antiques trade and salerooms offer opportunities to view and handle a considerable variety of pieces. However, the essence of both making a study and building a collection is selection, and this book attempts to guide readers to concentrate on and enjoy fine examples of needlework, pointing to special qualities within an outline of the history of the subject. Equally, it is hoped it may encourage modern embroiderers to undertake worth-while projects.

Because some aspects of needlework are virtually independent subjects in themselves, needing lengthy discussion, and since this book must have limits, they are reluctantly omitted from this study, except for points of general reference. Lace and Chinese embroidery are thus only mentioned occasionally and the wide field of costume is only discussed where its decoration is closely linked to the history of needlework. Needlepoint lace is, of course, a form of needlework but is traditionally considered with bobbin lace as a separate craft. Its influences on other needlework are however noted.

Chinese embroidery is certainly a world of its own, culturally far removed from Western styles. It fascinated early travellers and successive merchants but European reflections have always had a distinctive character, never seriously adopting the philosophical grammar of Chinese forms and symbolism, or attempting to emulate the minuteness of workmanship. As early as the 2nd century the Chinese were a source of wonder for 'precious figured garments resembling in colours the

Figure 1
German whitework known as *Point de Saxe* or Dresden lace with an extensive variety of patterned fillings, *c*.1770.

flowers of the field, and rivalling in fineness the work of spiders'. Over many centuries Chinese styles and techniques have changed relatively little; a classical form had emerged early on and, being an entirely satisfactory and significant aspect of that great country's way of life, it was on an elevated plane not subject to much variation. It was certainly wholly independent of European fashions, apart from items specially made for export. On the whole it is best left for separate consideration elsewhere.

Some passing references are made to needlework from each continent with a few linkings to ethnic and traditional forms but, again, these are limited to cases with relevance to the art-craft in the Western world.

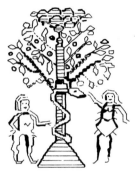

The Bible tells us that Adam and Eve sewed fig leaves together at the beginning of time, but whether it was sewing or weaving that was first developed is largely a matter of conjecture. Textile scholars are divided on this question; both techniques were practised long before the invention of thread or its application to other pliable materials, and they differ distinctly, with contrasting methods of manufacture. There is some confusion between tapestry weaving and needlework; we are concerned here with the latter, sewing, for though weaving is related, and woven materials usually provide the fabric on which needlework is done, the method of workmanship is entirely different. Weaving, as in the making of tapestries, is done on a loom with many threads being fed into it simultaneously, while needlework, as the word implies, is carried out with a needle and a single thread. The word tapestry is often loosely and incorrectly applied to canvas needlework. The tapestry weaving process is complex and expensive and was chiefly employed for making large pictorial hangings. Needlework, on the other hand, is based on the simple craft of sewing, with at times a wide variety of stitchery. Although some of the finest embroidery was made professionally, much is domestic in character, reflecting homely uses and personal designs and workmanship.

The earliest needlework was of a plain, practical nature, done with strong fibrous materials such as hair, to join skins and furs for clothing, and embroidery was used to strengthen parts subject to greater wear. From this humble origin a sumptuous decorative art gradually emerged. The words needlework and embroidery are nearly synonymous. The former is general, embracing in its widest sense ordinary work such as knitting, darning and seam making but it also includes embroidery, which more specifically suggests decoration or ornament. In old records, 'embroidery' normally refers to work in silks. But, as in the title of this book, 'needlework' often refers generally to decorative stitchery. The term 'needlepoint' is applied in America to canvas work, but earlier it referred to the sewing of lace made with a needle rather than bobbins. It may also be noted here that metal threads were 'wrought' while wools, in crewel embroidery or tent stitch, were 'worked'.

The primarily practical nature of needlework has held a disciplinary brake on decorative fantasies, curbing it within useful strictures. Its

Plate 2
Portrait of Elizabeth Vernon, Countess of Southampton, *c.*1620 showing examples of fine embroidered costume, accurately portrayed.

first purpose was always to provide clothing, both plain and ceremonial:

No surplice white the priest could wear
Bandless the bishop must appear
The King without a shirt would be
Did not the needle help all three.
(Mary Miller's sampler, 1735)

From this arose opportunities for very elaborate costume, reaching especially glorious heights in mediaeval religious and secular garments, in Tudor court dress and in 18th-century costume. The early use of quilting for protection and warmth developed into intricate decorative work and the need for personal colours for identification in mediaeval military encounters led to magnificent heraldic embroidery for the battlefield and court functions. The 17th century witnessed the use of fine needlework for newly sought household comforts, hangings and upholstery. New forms of fashionable costume and formal dress developed rapidly throughout the 17th, 18th and 19th centuries. Additional sewing in the form of samplers, pictures and objects was related to the general delight in making personal and domestic articles of either a utilitarian or a decorative nature.

Every country and race, and both rich and poor have enjoyed traditions of needlework, some very sophisticated, some naive but charming, and some with ancient roots. There is a unifying strand of charm which is conjured up through a fusion of traditional techniques and forms with occasional adaptations brought about by the availability of new materials or influence from other crafts. A certain warm naivity is a notable feature and a characteristic language of motifs. The absurdity of huge fishes being clearly depicted in tiny pools, streams or fountains

Figure 2
The Cope of the Passion, English *c.*1300, a magnificent example of *opus anglicanum*. Figures, animals and birds are linked in wreaths and the background is all gold like gilt metal or gilded furniture.

xii

is, for example, a long standing convention which can only delight. Even more strange is the slightly angular drawing of figures or foliage, emphasising the problems of stitching over regularly woven materials, which became a necessity and essential good manners in needlework.

Over the last five centuries we have been able to draw upon materials from world trade, and this has naturally shaped local production. Italy's trading in Mediterranean and Adriatic ports preceded oriental imports and created a basis for supremacy in making high quality textiles. In France and Italy fairly uniform techniques were established; the use of materials and designs followed a predictable formality appropriate to both countries' aristocratic patronage. English needlework, however, followed trends relatively independent of those of the continent. In the Middle Ages England produced vestments of unparalleled beauty but later products never attained such an elevated style or format. There was instead a tendency to soften influences of formal design and a delight in experimenting. Little prestige was attached to domestic embroidery, and fashions are seen to have been slow-moving, partly bound unashamedly to adaptations of old conventions but also subject sometimes to whims of the moment, and generally full of variety and life.

Often erroneously thought of as a humble and homely craft, needlework was in fact expensive, requiring costly materials, and was practised by queens and those from the highest ranks of society. The professionals of the craft were always highly rewarded. In a Greek poem of the 12th century Theodorus Prodromos says that if he had followed the embroiderers' trade his cupboard would have been full of bread, wine and sardines.[1] Henry III paid an embroideress the large sum of £11 for a chasuble and altar-piece; he clearly respected her as he subsequently paid her a visit when she retired to Bury St Edmunds.[2]

Contrary to Tennyson's epithet, 'Man for the sword and for the needle she', much mediaeval English needlework was done by men in workshops. Their craft was highly organised, exceptionally skilful and, above all, artistic in design and execution; the work became famed as *opus anglicanum* throughout Europe and was widely exported.

Inevitably, the styles of ecclesiastical vestments were continuously influenced by architecture. Romanesque arches and roundels formed the basic framing for hieratic figures. Later a tree of Jesse motif and elements of Decorated Gothic were adopted from architectural tracery. The finest artists drew out the designs, and cross-currents of mood can be noted in illumination, stained glass, metalwork, carving and enamels. Following the 14th century, when English vestments had passed their best, fine fabrics from continental Europe, such as velvets, damasks and brocades, relegated embroidery to smaller areas on orphreys, bands and roundels. Amongst painters who made designs for embroiderers were Sandro Botticelli (1440–1510) and Albrecht Dürer (1471–1528). A drawing by the latter for the hood of a cope is in the Victoria and Albert Museum. It depicts the Assumption of the Virgin and her Coronation.

Figure 3
Detail of an orphrey showing St Catherine, English *c.*1320.

Later the nobility employed artists to design amateur works for them. Catherine de Medici for example had an attendant designer called Federic di Vinciolo; he was author of an influential pattern book, *Les Singuliers et Nouveaux Pourtraicts et Ouvrages de Lingerie* (1587).

Fearful plagues, which devastated the craftsmen's communities, and the political and religious upheaval of the Reformation brought the flowering of ecclesiastical needlework to a final close. The Field of the Cloth of Gold tournament in 1520 coincided with a great transition to new materials. At this historic event Henry VIII and Francis I met *en fête* with huge supporting forces of courtiers and militia. The tournament took its name from the impressive spectacle of a dazzling mass of cloth of gold fabric, the ultimate of extravagance and worldly show.

The Tudor period, as we shall see, was especially rich in costume and domestic embroidery and some of it was well documented. The 'Inventair of the Queenis [Mary Queen of Scots] Movables, November 1561, at the Palace of Haleyrudehous' enumerates twelve 'beddis maid in broderie' of extraordinary richness. It is recorded that in 1582 at Sheffield Castle, the Earl of Shrewsbury had eighty-two feather beds. Another invaluable descriptive record was made by Paul Hentzner, giving details of his travels in the 1590's. On visiting the Tower of London, for example, he saw all sorts of embroidered beds, garments and items of which we now have little knowledge such as 'sadles of velvet of different colours'. Elizabeth I was given an embroidered saddle amongst the customary New Year gifts in 1588–9. Paintings of the period portray magnificent costumes, but it is interesting that even as late as 1598 a foreign visitor remarked on the lack of floor coverings, saying that even the Presence Chamber of Queen Elizabeth at Greenwich was 'strewn with hay'.[3]

Many late-16th- and 17th-century needlework designs were in the form of neat scrolling curls, or hoops, comparable with, for example, certain metalwork patterns such as the interlaced rings forming Boris Godunov's armour.[4] The needlework roundels were of open-ended foliate sprigs, incorporating flowers and insects in bright silks and metals or in 'cole black silks'[5] as worn by the Miller's wife in Chaucer. Flowers in contrasting moods indicate swings of taste and fashion. Tudor and Stuart flowers were accurately depicted representations of specially cultivated specimens, and were increasingly worked into scrolling patterns, the formation of which became as important as the individual depiction. In the 17th century, real flowers were still portrayed, but even more deliberately as specimen 'slips', or sprigs, and in sprays and group arrangements. Unreal, exotic foliage and blooms of oriental origin were a feature of crewelwork at the end of the century, and during the first half of the 18th. From the 1730s floral needlework, in tent and cross stitch on canvas, depicted natural garden blooms in controlled groupings. This was suited to carpets, chair seats and other furniture. By the end of the century many more arrangements were embroidered,

Plate 3a (top)
Part of a large 17th-century bed cover, perhaps Portuguese, decorated with raised strapwork. (11 ft 3 in x 10 ft).

Plate 3b (bottom)
Detail of a Queen Anne coverlet showing a vine-like pattern on a 'false quilted' silk ground.

xiv

Figure 4
One of a series of
Austrian wall and bed
hangings in the manner
of Jean Bérain, of chintz
appliqué and embroidery,
c. 1725.

with precision and naturalism, in fine silks; these were gathered in baskets, vases, or neat posies tied by a ribbon. Further exotic and unreal chinoiserie flowers and fruit were depicted in late-Georgian and late-Regency designs but all were swept aside in the 19th century by garish and blowsy blooms of often grossly stitched Berlin work. Throughout three centuries however, gardening and needlework reflected comparable joys, in layout, colouring and selection; the two pastimes were frequently discussed in similar terms:

> What greater delight is there than to behold the earth apparelled with plants, as with a robe of imbroidered works, set with orient pearles and garnished with great diversitie of rare and costly jewels.
>
> *John Gerard's* Herbal *1597*

Fashions generally, having reached certain conventions, changed slowly, and most needlework followed traditional forms without startling novelty or originality. The Oxburgh hangings (*Plate 12*), for

xvi

Figure 5 a & b
A pair of German
beadwork panels by Von
Selow of Brunswick,
showing formal gardens,
*c.*1730.

example, worked by Mary Queen of Scots and Elizabeth Shrewsbury, are amongst our finest treasures, though the designs and the technique were far from new. Their great charm rests in a combination of good drawing and colouring with interesting shapes, curious subjects and engaging emblems, specially charged with historical associations.

Injections of influence were brought to England with the arrival of the Houses of Orange and Hanover in 1688 and 1714. Queen Mary, who ruled with William III, was, it is said, more often seen with a skein of thread about her neck than attending to State affairs. Among a number of hangings worked by her was a set for a bed at Hampton Court referred to by Daniel Defoe as 'of her own work, while in Holland, very magnificent'.[6]

At the French court, Madame de Maintenon was equally passionate about needlework and is said to have done it while travelling in her carriage. Building at Versailles was carried out for Louis XIV to a scale and excellence never before attempted and architecture influenced every element of the decorative arts. Charles Le Brun supervised the mammoth schemes of interior decoration, and sumptuous textiles added both richness and softness to the monumental apartments. In England and France, luxurious comfort was achieved in the warmth of hangings, noble beds and rich upholstery. French craftsmen with a wide variety of needle skills were well ordered in guilds pertaining to their roles, and these co-ordinated high standards. They included *chasubliers, brodeurs, tailleurs, lingères* and *tapissiers* (upholsterers). The Broderers' Company in London incorporated most of these departments including the last, especially important suppliers, and was a powerful organisation. The haberdasher who supplied materials, equipment and contacts with professional designers was a significant link in all the businesses, and we note in *The Canterbury Tales* that the haberdashers, weavers and dyers were all wealthy merchants. Political and trade rulings, enforced through legal restrictions, were made from time to time but were usually short-lived attempts to encourage or curb fashions and crafts. These included a limitation on imports of inexpensive oriental needlework and the forbidding of the manufacture of embroidered and cloth-covered buttons, to boost the trade of metal button makers.

Eighteenth-century needlework was often bright and delicate, with clarity and line like a beautiful singing voice. The ancient skill of quilting was adapted to wonderfully decorative effects especially on coverlets or 'counterpanes', a word derived from the quilting stitch *contre pointe*. Samplers became essentially quaint and decorative and bridged a gap between costume and pictures, though their original use was associated with learning the skills of sewing. Later ones are now more generally appreciated than the finer early ones which are seldom seen; many later ones have a pleasing charm and alluring sentimental qualities. Most have texts indicating the combination of learning moral lessons alongside stitchery, as in Mary Cole's of 1759:

xvii

Better by Far for Me
Than all the Simpsters Art
That God's Commandments be
Embroider'd on my Heart.

The progression of pictorial motifs arrived at a significant format around the 1730s. Mediaeval embroidery had been largely narrative but since then the depiction of human activities, animals and scenes had been in the form of isolated figures. 'Spot' motifs without link or relationship were a characteristic feature of the 17th century. But in the 18th century there was an increased delight in pictorial composition, at first incorporating the creatures and conventions tried out in the tent stitch and stumpwork pictures of previous generations, but then with fresh and more united themes. Rustic scenes with stylised shepherds, shepherdesses and sheep were amongst the most popular subjects as well as new renderings of the ever-suitable but more ponderous myths, fables and Bible stories. All these found their way onto needlework upholstery. Each developed ultimately into silk and wool pictures, depicted in less appropriate neo-classical terminology. Human faces always presented a major challenge to needleworkers and latterly the struggle was abandoned in favour of painting in the finer details and backgrounds. The development of pictorial design clearly reflects the general changes of taste and fashion throughout the century—the baroque giving way to lighter rococo elements, including separate and combined oriental and Gothic trends, and then the exclusion of these for neo-classicism. Baroque needlework seems like a flourish of joy with a confident quality akin to Bach's Brandenburg concertos, while rococo, at best, has the predicable precision, delicacy and perpetual novelty of Mozart.

Much needlework of the late 18th and 19th centuries was unremarkable; it tended to imitate the *métier* of painting and engraving rather than have its own character. Other crafts, however, such as the weaving of

Figure 6
Seat for a settee with scenes derived from William Kent's illustrations to Gay's Fables, *c*.1730.

Plate 4
Detail of late 17th-century English crewel-work bed hangings showing considerable oriental influence.

Figure 7
One of a pair of French
silk pictures, largely in
chenille stitch and the
vase highlighted with
gold thread, *c.*1830
(20 in x 16 in).

Figure 8
Detail of ballooning
picture worked in chain
and other stitches,
French, *c.*1790.
(9½ in x 7 in).

carpets mirrored some of the finer traits of design and even copied the
look of stitchery. Locally produced and imported rugs, Axminster and
Bessarabian for example, were successfully based on needlework patterns
and a sewing tradition was carried along through these with a tendency
to coarser workmanship.

Berlin woolwork was the first main innovation of the 19th century,
being established first in Germany and then brought to England around
1820. It was a further form of needlepainting. Thousands of printed and
coloured patterns, mostly in the form of pictures, some after old masters
or popular modern painters, were produced on squared paper that
indicated each stitch for canvas embroidery. Originally published in
Berlin, they were available at Mr Wilks' shop in Regent Street, London
by 1831, together with soft, brightly coloured merino wools, also
imported from Germany. There was on the whole little artistry in this
embroidery, although in some cases ladies invented ingenious tasks with
greater originality, normally for 'useful' household items, and sometimes on a large scale. (*Plate 28a*)

The other kind of needlework which was massively produced in the
first half of the 19th century was Ayrshire whitework. Tens of thousands
of impoverished women in Scotland and Northern Ireland were employed in their own homes, at the organised industrial production of
children's clothes, aprons, bonnets and other garments of light cotton
muslin elaborately 'flowered' with white embroidery. Much of the work
was exported to England, Europe and America. The central co-ordinat-

Figure 9
Woolwork picture of a
parrot, a rosebush and
strawberries worked on
felt, *c.*1830.

ing workshops and businesses were comparable with the needlework industry that exported vestments in the Middle Ages.

It was in reaction to the sterile success of these two 19th-century mainstreams, and the technical complacency of the Great Exhibition of 1851 that William Morris and other craft-orientated designers broke away from the inevitable mechanisation of needlework. They sought wholly hand-made, individual, even idiosyncratic hallmarks in both technique and design. In doing this they first turned to a revival of mediaeval forms as well as adapting elements of Persian design. Huge leaf patterns were tried out alongside colourful Gothic constructions. They were heavily graceful and laden with ornate detailing, quite unlike the elegant mediaeval originals or Georgian revivals from which they were derived. Other designs were supplied by leading painters.

Too busy a combination of decorative elements, or too many stitch varieties, or colours, weakens design. It was in this respect that much Victorian needlework failed to have significant lasting qualities. Earlier and finer pieces show how a certain simplicity and control are crucial factors of success. Today a sense of 'good taste' prevails over the specialist scholarship and depth of knowledge that were signal hallmarks of late Victorian and Edwardian England. The trend is partly a healthy one, but true connoisseurship should combine both; we have now strayed so far from a learned approach with a traditional grounding in Classical, historical and religious culture that we almost neglect our inherited background, and are in danger of severing the cord of continuity that must run into the creation of modern works. Needlework, however, has fortunately always been related to the production of practical artefacts:

> Untill the world be quite dissolv'd and past
> So long at least the needles use shall last.

From such a traditional basis there is wide scope for interesting new developments.

Restoring, and the conservation of old and valuable pieces, was in mediaeval times one of the chief duties of convents and workshops; today this is again one of the most seriously considered tasks of needlewomen. New theories and techniques to match them will, it is hoped, help to preserve for us the great heritage that we have in Great Britain, Europe and the United States of America.

NOTES

Dedication page epigram: *Rom. I 20* (Revised Version)

Epigram: *Spectator*, 1714.

1 *Apollo* January, 1977, p. 57.

2 Ibid.

3 M. J. Mayorcas, *English Needlework Carpets*, 1963, p. 9.

4 Kremlin Museum, Moscow.

5 Chaucer, *The Miller's Tale*.

6 Queen Anne was also an embroideress. See a sale catalogue of Hall Waterbridge and Owen, Auctioneers, in the Music Hall, Shrewsbury, Sept. 18th 1875, Lot 151: 'A fine piece of Old Silk tapestry—a garden scene, the offerings of Flora to Venus . . . etc. This screen, the work of Queen Anne, was presented by Her Majesty to the Rt. Hon. Richard Hill, Ambassador Extraordinary to the Court of Turin, 1703.' Mentioned by a correspondent to *Country Life*, Nov. 29th, 1956.

1 Early Needlework

First look at the embroideries, delicate and so charming;
you would say they were the robes of the gods.

THE GODDESS Athena is said to have taught our cultural ancestors, the Greeks, the art of embroidery. The specific origins of the craft are almost entirely lost; the few remaining threads of historical fact are sufficient only for qualified conjecture.

Unfortunately, the blessings of a temperate climate here in the West do not provide the phenomenon of perpetual preservation which some cultures have known, and few significant archaeological specimens have been preserved. In South America, Indian embroideries of the 5th century B.C. have been found in considerable quantities in funerary bundles, and a fragment of Greek needlework of the same period has also survived. Likewise very early ornamental sewing was discovered in the frozen tombs of Russia, but our textile history cannot be traced back further than the early Middle Ages.

Fragments of evidence show that attempts to decorate cloth may have preceded other skills and may have influenced other awakening art forms. Early Egyptians imitated embroidery in paintings and it is thought that their love of colour in enamels, metals and glass was inspired by textiles and dyes. The Phoenicians, whose territory, on the maritime border of Palestine, became a province of Egypt, were extensive travellers, and spread ideas gathered from different parts of the world. In about 1650 B.C. they brought the arts and crafts of Babylon and Assyria across Europe to England in their search for tin. They were highly successful merchants of luxuries and traded above all in Tyre purple, procured from the shellfish *murex* of Mediterranean shores. This brought them great wealth, as it was indispensable to the pomp of sacerdotal and imperial ceremonial. Variations of the colour are still symbolic of the hierarchy of Church and State.

The Romans' continuous conquests in Europe and repeated invasions of Britain brought new aspects of craftsmanship and introduced Christianity. They did not find this island easy to govern, often because of their own injustice. In A.D. 62 they were faced with a colossal rebellion led by Boadicea whose huge number of supporters were brutally crushed. It is said that Boadicea herself was captured wearing a fur-lined mantle of embroidered skins. This garment was probably not unlike ones still made by Eskimos and North American Indians.

Figure 10
A woolwork roundel, 7th-10th century, found in burial grounds in Egypt and depicting the Annunciation and Visitation. (Diameter about 8½ in).

Christianity, propagated by the Romans in the early Middle Ages, that is from about the 7th century A.D., became the chief stimulus of artistic effort and expression. St Augustine, who is credited with the conversion of the Britons, carried with him a banner embroidered with the image of Christ.

When the power of Rome declined, the far lying island of Britain was left to invasion by Celts, Saxons and Vikings (known here as the Danes), but despite considerable strife and pillaging the country eventually settled down to relative prosperity. Early in the 7th century Aldhelm, Bishop of Sherborne, wrote a poem mentioning tapestry weaving and embroidery, worked by the women of England. From early on until the height of the mediaeval period, when highly organised professional workshops consisted of male needleworkers, embroidery was chiefly the cherished prowess of Anglo-Saxon women. It was done especially by those of noble and privileged position. St Etheldreda, Abbess and patron saint of Ely (died 679) offered St Cuthbert a stole and maniple

2

Figure 11
Peter the Deacon and St
John the Baptist on part
of the maniple of St
Cuthbert, originally
ordered for Frithestan,
Bishop of Winchester by
Queen Ælfflæd, *c*.910.

finely embroidered by herself and worked with gold and precious stones. She was also known by the name of St Audrey, from which the word *tawdry*, used to describe a cheap kind of lace purchasable at St Audrey's Fair, was derived. Another early gift was that of Wiklaf, King of Mercia, who presented to the abbey of Croyland, in 833, a cloak embroidered with the battle of Troy.

The earliest surviving piece of needlework in Western Europe is the much deteriorated but interesting remnant of an English chasuble at Maeseyck in Belgium. Though now only a glorious ruin, it has been treasured as a relic of two female saints, St Harlindis and St Relindis. Of Anglo-Saxon workmanship in the second half of the 9th century, it must once have been spectacular, with coloured silks, gilt thread and seed pearls depicting birds, animals and monograms in interlacing roundels. The design appears to be related to the illumination of manuscripts. Monks and priests were closely involved with the maintenance and decoration of their magnificent buildings and they participated in the production of manuscripts and vestments. The 10th-century Archbishop of Canterbury, St Dunstan, is known to have designed embroideries.

Remarkable and beautiful survivals of about 915 are a stole and maniple discovered in 1827 in the tomb of St Cuthbert at Durham Cathedral. Both have inscriptions indicating that they were made for Queen Ælfflæd, wife of Edward the Elder, for Bishop Frithestan of Winchester. They were probably made in that city, then the Saxon capital. Different in style from the Maeseyck chasuble, they depict saints with the inscriptions; the stole is embroidered with the *Agnus Dei*, and the maniple with the hand of God issuing from clouds. The figures on both pieces are finely worked but are of a stiff hieratic nature, Byzantine in feeling, and showing no signs of the expressiveness that was to be the special characteristic of later English work.

Much fine needlework must have been made outside monastic circles for ecclesiastical, semi-ecclesiastical or wholly secular uses. Queen Emma, wife firstly of Ethelred the Unready (died 1016), and secondly of King Canute (died 1036), embroidered many vestments and altar cloths. The latter King's second wife, Queen Ælgiva, gave amongst other gifts an altar hanging with a gold border to the Abbey of Ely; their daughter Æthelswitha also practised gold embroidery.

Of work of a ceremonial nature, we are informed in the writings of William of Malmesbury that King Edward the Confessor's wife Editha (or Ædgytha) embroidered the mantle for his coronation in 1042. Queen Margaret, wife of Malcolm III of Scotland, was also a skilled needlewoman, embroidering various vestments and hangings.

Heraldic needlework, too, was firmly established; William of Malmesbury again records that King Harold went to the Battle of Hastings with a banner embroidered with a fighting man, worked in gold and enriched with precious stones.

3

THE BAYEUX TAPESTRY

By far the most remarkable embroidery of the early Middle Ages to have survived is the so-called Bayeux 'Tapestry'. Though not of outstanding workmanship, its historical nature and charm make it justly famous. Two hundred and thirty feet (70 m) long, by about twenty inches (50 cm) high, it consists of a long narrative wall hanging made up of joined parts, probably separately worked by professional teams.

Narrative historical hangings were very much part of the tradition of European needlework but no others have survived. Old texts give us some insight such as the Scandinavian *Völsunga Saga* which includes a description of Brynhild in her bower at Hlymdale: 'overlaying cloth with gold, and sewing therein the great deeds which Sigmund had wrought, the slaying of the Worm, and the taking of the wealth of him, and the death of Regin withal'.

The relatively simple needlework of the Bayeux Tapestry is in coloured wools of eight shades: blues, greens, yellow and terracotta red. The hanging is representative of ecclesiastical and non-ecclesiastical decorations of the period and has probably survived due to the fact that no gold was employed but only simple materials. Others of finer workmanship and precious materials are known to have existed. An account by Baudri, Abbot of Bourgueil, described, for example, a much more elaborate 'tapestry' telling the same story, hung around an alcove as bed hangings for Adela, daughter of William the Conqueror:

> A wonderful tapestry goes around the lady's bed, which joins three things in material and novel skill. For the hand of craftsmen hath done the work so finely that you would scarcely believe that to exist which you know does exist. Threads of gold come first, silver threads come next, the third set of threads were always of silk. Skilful care had made the threads of gold and silver so fine that I believe that nothing could have been thinner.... Jewels with red marking were shining amidst the work, and pearls of no small price. In fine so great was the glitter and beauty of the tapestry that you might say it surpassed the rays of Phoebus.[1]

Figure 12
A section from the Bayeux Tapestry showing Harold returning to England, riding to London and visiting King Edward at Westminster.

4

Figure 13
Another part of the
Bayeux Tapestry showing
Duke William (extreme
left) exhorting his soldiers
at the Battle of Hastings,
1066.

Almost a hundred years earlier, it was recorded that Æthelflæd embroidered the deeds of her husband Britnoth on a hanging which she gave to the Abbey of Ely, probably shortly after his death in 991.[2]

The Bayeux Tapestry was made between the time of these two others, in about 1070, to commemorate the Norman Conquest of Britain and, specifically, the Battle of Hastings. It was probably commissioned by Odo, Bishop of Bayeux, the powerful half-brother of William the Conqueror, for the new cathedral dedicated in 1077, or for use in a castle. The workmanship appears to be English and the lively design was probably drawn out by an illuminator of manuscripts, perhaps at Canterbury; conventions of manuscript illustration are reflected in border patterns and a diagrammatic portrayal of architecture. Apart from these aspects, there is an extraordinary wealth of detail displaying the genius of an observant and knowledgeable man. A Latin text describes the action, and from a Norman point of view tells the history of the invasion, Harold's defeat, and his death at the Battle of Hastings. The tale lays unexpected emphasis on Harold's visit to Normandy and his swearing allegiance to Duke William as heir to the English throne, which is strange since Harold was a natural enemy of the French. Concisely, the story related by the embroidery is as follows.

Edward the Confessor briefs Harold who is then seen setting out for France with falcon and hounds. He prays at a church at Bosham and sails off for France. On arrival he is immediately arrested and taken prisoner. He is taken to Duke William of Normandy and the two are seen together in the latter's palace. They go on an expedition to Brittany where Harold rescues two soldiers from quicksand. They engage in the siege of Dinant and defeat Conan. Harold is honoured by William in a ceremony, ranking between knighthood and enrolment as a supporter of William, and subsequently they go to Bayeux where Harold makes an oath of allegiance to William. Harold returns to England and reports at Westminster to Edward who is on his deathbed. We then see the King's funeral procession. Harold is crowned forthwith as his successor and is told of a comet. In Normandy William holds a council, prepares to sail for England and sets out in splendid boats. He hurries to Hastings where

various domestic arrangements are made, and a feast and council are held. Harold and William prepare for and lead their armies to battle and they attack each other ferociously. Harold's brothers are killed and also many men and horses. Bishop Odo is seen cheering on his troops. Harold is wounded in the eye and finally the English are seen fleeing.

A small part is probably missing at the end but in all an extraordinary cross-section of life is portrayed. Some 600 figures are shown and many more animals, birds and fishes. Members of the two ruling households are depicted with interesting views of buildings including the Palace and Abbey at Westminster. The needlework serves as a document for social historians as it records many kinds of clothing for battle, peacetime, and church use, as well as activities such as farming, hunting, shipbuilding, cooking and the appearance of Halley's comet. The drawing and stitching convey extraordinary liveliness and variety of movement, and though restored at least twice, the needlework is in very good condition.

Under the influence of the Normans the development of underside couching, whereby laid threads were secured to the surface by a slighter thread pulling them through from the back of the material, meant that designs could be more flexible and free flowing. This led to the special expressiveness of English mediaeval needlework.

William the Conqueror's chaplain and chronicler, William de Poitiers, recorded that after the conquest the French took home magnificent English embroidered state robes, far finer than they had seen before. They presented vestments to churches in Normandy and William's wife, Queen Matilda, bequeathed English needlework to the Church of the Holy Trinity at Caen, one piece embroidered at Winchester. She gave her golden mantle to be made into a cope and her girdle for suspending the lamp before the high altar. These gifts are an indication of the great value put on precious textiles.

Shortly after the Conquest, William I instigated a colossal survey (1085–87) to assess the nation's worth. This invaluable record, the Domesday Book, mentions fascinating day-to-day facts and arrange-

Details from the border of the Bayeux Tapestry.

ments such as the granting of land to a woman referred to as 'Aldwid the maiden' by a sheriff Godric, as a reward for teaching his daughter the art of gold embroidery.

Embroidery had already taken a position of high status: it was held in higher esteem than painting and illumination, both of which were influenced by it. It continued to be the favourite pursuit of Anglo-Norman ladies, as well as being practised professionally in workshops, and in church and secular institutions. Very high standards of design and workmanship were expected and certainly achieved.

NOTES

Epigram: Theocritus, *Idyll XV*. Embroidered on a screen designed by Walter Crane, at the London School of Economics.

1 Quoted in 'The Bayeux Tapestry in the hands of Restorers', Charles Dawson, F. S. A. (*The Antiquary*, August 1907) and by Margaret Jourdain, *English Secular Embroidery*, 1910.

2 A. F. Kendrick, *English Needlework*, 1933.

2 The Mediaeval Period

Pen of Steele and Silken incke enroll'd

IT IS A TOO little known fact, and certainly no exaggeration, that one of England's greatest cultural achievements and contributions to world art has been her production of superb ecclesiastical vestments, particularly between 1250 and 1350. Known as *opus anglicanum* (English work), the magnificent products of Winchester, London and elsewhere were the envy of cathedrals, churches and private chapels all over Europe. Costly items were ordered and exported in surprisingly large numbers.

This mediaeval needlework was of a remarkably high quality in both design and technique and it is not surprising that English pieces became traditionally prized by continental neighbours. The religious designs were executed in a natural manner and characterised by needlepainting or acupictura; altar frontals and vestments portrayed statuesque figures representing the saints in perfect detail and with delicate paintbrush accuracy. They shared features in common with manuscript illumination, since the ablest artists of the period provided designs for both crafts; it is indeed known that two 13th-century French embroideresses, Dame Margot and Dame Aalès were themselves also illuminators. Needlework techniques influenced painting and illumination and may have inspired stained glass. There are also parallels in Limoges enamelwork, bronze-work and ivory carving. The horizontal rows of saints in niches, familiar on altar frontals and in vertical columns on vestments, are undoubtedly associated with the architectural tiers of sculptures on the great cathedrals being built around this time.

Tapestry weaving was developed during the 12th century but it did not displace embroidery, for although it was sometimes used for the decoration of church walls it was not suitable for vestments. The great quantity of needlework that was made and treasured is indicated by the fact that over 600 vestments were listed in the inventory of Lincoln Cathedral, all embroidered, and some encrusted with jewels. There were also mitres, frequently of elaborate needlework, and sometimes bejewelled or decorated with seed pearls like a later one from the Sainte Chapelle, now in the Musée de Cluny.

As artistic decoration passed its zenith in the later Middle Ages, bolder but often less beautiful feats of the embroiderers' skill were displayed. Deep-relief padded work was perfected in Germany in the 15th century. The heavier forms of this appear cumbersome, though the

Plate 5
The choirs of angels on the back of a mid-13th-century chasuble, part of a complete set of vestments probably made by nuns for the doner Abbess Kunigunde II (1239-69), Göss Convent, near Leoben, Styria, Austria.

9

Figure 14
Norwegian wall hanging
(detail) worked in
coloured wools. Early
13th century.

intricate backgrounds of couched-down gold thread, sometimes in
elaborate geometric patterns, are delightful and are clearly associated
with the exact chasing and engraving of goldsmiths' work. The technique was known as *or de Chypre*.

While ecclesiastical needlework has survived relatively well, probably
since it was cherished for both its temporal and spiritual values, there
was also much secular needlework which has not survived. I shall refer
to aspects of magnificent costume and heraldry later, but more practical
forms of needlework were relatively simple and plain. The ancient art of
quilting had been used in China as protection from the cold and early
on as a form of armour, and later as a lining for armour. It was used
extensively in Arabia and Persia where crusaders saw it and adopted it
between the 11th and 15th centuries. A similar form is still used for
armour in Nigeria, where Fulani warriors wear it and drape it over their
horses for protection.

From about the time of the Norman conquest of Britain, the Romanesque
style was prevalent throughout Europe but did not leave very strong
marks in needlework. However, an English piece at Sens Cathedral is a
good example of the simple interlocking hoop and round-arch patterns
that were the essence of decoration within that architectural style.

In the meantime, the tradition of narrative wall hangings, like the
Bayeux Tapestry, was continued in several countries. In Norway, for
example, an interesting hanging from Höylandet of about 1230 depicts
the three magi in processional form. Undoubtedly the work of a professional workshop, it shares certain characteristics with the Bayeux
Tapestry, one being that it is worked in couched-down wools. The
linear forms of the figures and the horses are filled in with interesting
patterns giving a shaded effect. A fine secular survival is a wall hanging

from Lower Saxony of about 1300 depicting narrative scenes of the Tristan legend, interspersed with armorial shields. It recalls mediaeval poetry, especially Chaucer's *Canterbury Tales* and his long narrative poem *Troilus and Criseyde*.

Church needlework, however, remains predominant. We note that from the Norman Conquest there was a development in design from roundels to large scrolling forms, incorporating figures that were less statuesque and showed greater expression. Similarly, scenes were depicted in other linked patterns. An increased fluidity of style and an unsurpassed mastery of techniques combined to make English embroidery the envy of rich patrons throughout Europe. Pope Innocent III (1198–1216) saw certain vestments and orphreys and on being told that they originated in this country he exclaimed, 'Surely England must be a garden of delight!'

OPUS ANGLICANUM

The best English mediaeval needlework has never been equalled and is as much a wonder and treasured legacy as, for example, its architectural contemporary Chartres Cathedral. As a corpus it contains a seriousness and nobility on a level with the greatest music, perhaps Bach's *St Matthew Passion*; the two have much in common. Both combine religious narrative with an utter sensitivity of spirit. The embroideries were highly sophisticated, ahead of their time in many respects, and were indeed contemporary with the mere beginnings of musical notation.

The qualities of *opus anglicanum* were essentially twofold: firstly, the technical achievements were exceptional and were carried out with excellent materials; secondly, the designs, layout and religious portraiture were developed by the finest artists of the day, especially gifted men, admirably suited to their medium. The technique of using under-side couching, whereby gold and silk threads were attached to the material by small loops held through the material and secured on the back by another thread, meant that a great degree of flexibility in design was possible. Additionally, this made the finished article less stiff and cumbersome. The greater part of the embroidery worked in coloured silks was of fine split stitch, so minute that extraordinary accuracy could be attained in facial expressions and shading.

Overall designs developed through several basic forms. Flowing circles and geometric patterns in rows, each containing figures and scenes, provided the predominant format. Subsequently these became interlocking and more complex; many are comparable with the divisions of stained glass windows. Another contemporary plan in design was the tree of life, or stem of Jesse pattern, linking saints and vignettes like recitatives and arias within a general narrative framework. This age-old device had already been used in pictorial interpretation throughout the world and in many mediums. The ultimate method of linking subjects

and stories was to show them within an orderly framework of pointed
arches or niches, as depicted on the facades of Gothic cathedrals. These
might be placed in radiating arcs on a cope, in rows on an altar frontal,
or in vertical columns on an orphrey.

A glorious English cope of *c.*1300 at the cathedral of Saint-Bertrand-
de-Comminges, Haute-Garonne (*Fig. 2*) displays an infinite variety of
Passion scenes, the Ascension, the Pentecost and the Coronation of the
Virgin in roundels and oval medallions and also many birds and small
animals, all against a gold background.[1]

The Victoria and Albert Museum has fine examples of *opus anglicanum*. Though it should be remembered that inevitably every item has been cut and altered, sometimes drastically, each surviving piece is an enthralling and masterly jewel. The Steeple Aston cope pieces (*c*.1320) have a silver and olive mystery (*Plate 6*) while the orphrey parts are well preserved and full of the original life. The Clare chasuble, of a few decades earlier, is characterised by its blue satin ground over which are embroidered neat but languid scrolling tendrils containing animals. The front of this chasuble depicts a group of scenes in the cruciform pattern so frequently employed as a Christian ecclesiastical symbol. Based on the shape of a square, with arches on four sides, it was used at two different angles, diagonal and upright, with an effect that was curiously different, even magical. (*See diagram alongside*.) The base of church pillars have often been carved in this pattern.[2]

The beautiful Jesse cope (*c*.1300) with embroidery on red silk twill (*Plate 7*) shows elegantly, within a formalised tree-tendril pattern, his descendants stemming from his recumbent figure. The Syon cope is entirely covered with embroidery on linen and the design is composed of glorious figures within interlocking cruciform patterns, as above, at both angles. The orphrey and outer band depict heraldry. The Butler Bowden cope, of the second quarter of the 14th century, is an example of later *opus anglicanum*. Of a more complex design, perhaps less success-ful, the figures are enclosed by high-Gothic foliate arches while a long orphrey is of a stiff hieratic and jewel-like precision. A chasuble made

Figure 16
The Syon Cope. English, 1300–20. One of the finest survivals of *opus anglicanum*.

Figure 17
Orphrey cross, English
*c.*1320, with gold
background.

from a cope of a comparable form is in the Metropolitan Museum, New York.

A panel bearing the name John of Thanet, 'a Monk and Chaunter', mathematician and author, of Canterbury Cathedral, shows the enthroned Christ in unusually large format. He is holding the orb of the world which is incribed EVROPA AFF'CA ASIA. The blue silk background is 'powdered' with lions rampant in silver.

Several magnificent orphreys show charming figures against meticulously worked gold backgrounds, and usually within a variation of interweaving patterns. In contrast to these, but comparable with the Butler Bowden cope, is a fine band of the first half of the 14th century depicting scenes from the life of the Virgin worked in coloured silks and metal threads on red velvet. It seems at once full of spontaneous passion and timeless human expression. (*Plate 8b*)

By the 13th century the making of vestments had become an important and lucrative industry. There were in London, and elsewhere, many workshops of professional male embroiderers with critical standards of workmanship, and these flourished in catering for domestic and foreign orders, and for the requirements of rich city merchants. Some individual craftsmen were well known and sometimes embroiderers went abroad to undertake commissions. The high standard in English workshops was founded on seven-year apprenticeships and a continuity of experience. Nuns, too, carried out semi-professional work, under the guidance of professionals. Both did repairs and restoration work as well as new commissions.

Opus anglicanum was at its best from 1250 to 1350. The finest pieces display a wealth of incidental detail but (as in architecture) in a way that never diminishes from the main theme. Fine vestments were exported to Flanders, France and Italy and are to be found today in many European countries. The Vatican in Rome had more English needlework than any other, as shown in the 1295 inventory of the Holy See. Pope Boniface VIII made gifts of English embroidery to the cathedral of his birthplace, Anagni, in about 1300. He also gave a very fine altar frontal of an English type, though probably made in Rome, depicting two tiers of arches with saints in the upper, and Gospel scenes in the lower. The piece shows also a revival of Byzantine influences brought about by mosaic artists whose glittering masterpieces were done around Venice, and later in Rome.

The Black Death (1348) can roughly be said to mark the end of the flowering of *opus anglicanum*. It caused embroidery workshops, as all other trades, to be horribly decimated. Other deteriorating factors included strains on resources brought about by the Hundred Years War with France and the domestic unrest in England itself. Changes in techniques and materials, some of them quicker and cheaper, altered the especially English appearance of vestments. A greater use was made of fine, imported materials from Italy; superb velvets and brocades,

replacing plainer silks, were now used for the main body of copes and chasubles—needlework was limited to orphreys or to applied pieces. These consisted of stitching on fine linen which was then attached where necessary over the velvet pile. This new trend, concentrating more on fine fabrics, led to a different aspect of luxury and richness; elegant flowing robes of wonderful textures and colours replaced the jewel-like quality of dense pictorial needlework with its portrayal of scenes of harrowing religious passion. The weavers' art now rose to supremacy. Needlework became more formalised and stiff, unadventurously following continental conventions, including strapwork backgrounds. The remarkable draughtsmen had moved into other fields; figures were now pricked out and 'pounced'. Quicker and cheaper methods encouraged by excessive demands generally affected the quality of workmanship; long and short, brick and satin stitches often replaced finer varieties and surface couching was substituted for the more laborious underside couching. The characteristic tiny, split stitching of the 13th century was replaced by the use of stem stitch.

Increasingly, English workers followed European fashions with coarser, padded work and imitations of tapestry weaving. These were never of the highest quality but they enjoyed a wide popularity, the coarser embroidery ironically becoming known as *façon d'Angleterre*.

Or nué or 'shaded gold' was a significant technique. Probably orginating in Flanders but much used in many parts of Europe, it allowed for a new versatility in needlepainting. The principle was a simple one: gold threads were couched-down horizontally by irregularly placed coloured silk threads which gave a shaded effect according to their density, as in painting, against the metallic surface. The strictly horizontal lines of the gold gave an impression of weaving so that the embroidery resembled tapestry; this aspect also eliminated the multiple reflections of light previously caused by threads being laid at different angles. A fine example of the technique is a group of twenty-seven pieces in the Museum of Santa Maria del Fiore in Florence. These are after designs made for vestments by Antonio del Pollaiuolo (1431–98) and are very well documented. The technique of *or nué* continued in use well into the 17th century, and was used by Charles I's embroiderer.

In France, the ancient method of couching wool, *point couché*, (as in the Bayeux Tapestry) continued throughout the Middle Ages and appliqué, or applied work, was also popular. St Louis (1215–1270) of France sent the Tartar King a set of vestments and other church furnishings depicting Gospel scenes in applied work. Raised and padded *broderie en relief* was also done.

Flanders was latterly an important centre of European embroidery and weaving. Its long tradition of these is seen in the rich and heavy draperies depicted in Flemish painting. An interesting group of embroideries associated with the story of St Martin, of the early or mid-15th century, is attributed to a Franco-Flemish origin. Formerly part of an altar frontal, a cope, or a set of vestments, the pieces consist chiefly of thirty-three roundels illustrating events in the life of St Martin, though the incident of his dividing his cloak to share it with a beggar is missing. The embroideries have great charm and are shared by the Musée Historique des Tissus at Lyons and the Metropolitan Museum in New York.

Several South German vestments survive from the reign of Henry II (died 1024); they are of fine workmanship and closely associated in design with Regensburg illumination, and show also Byzantine influence. They are largely of gold, couched onto silk, such as the mantle of St Cunegund decorated with a large number of medallions portraying saints and narrative scenes. There was also in Germany a strong tradition from mediaeval times of whitework embroidery, *opus teutonicum*; fine altar frontals, veils and hangings of simple and cheap materials contrasted sharply with the extravagance of the gold embroidery.

Later German and Austrian needlework was very sculptural. Raised and padded parts appear to imitate features of metalwork and carved wood. Pieces of wood were actually incorporated for relief effects under the needlework. (This was no doubt the origin of the stumpwork that became a short-lived but exuberant craze in 17th-century England.) German and Austrian orphreys in cross form, for example, frequently showed the crucified Christ in deep relief, supported at the extremities of the arms by angels and with God the Father, or saints, or Christ rising from the tomb, above and below, in the same technique. Vestments were often further enriched with pearls and precious stones.

A remarkable, complete set of 13th-century Austrian vestments is preserved in Vienna. Of late Romanesque style and worked in coloured

Figure 19
Franco-Flemish chasuble cross with roundels depicting events in the life of St Martin, *c.*1440.

silks, they depict choirs of angels under round arches, animal symbols, geometric key patterns and God enthroned in a starry sky within a circle. This last symbol would again seem to be of a Byzantine origin. From the former convent of Göss, near Leoben, in Styria, the vestments consist of all five major items: cope, chasuble (*Plate 5*), dalmatic, tunicle and altar frontal. They were made for the abbess of the convent, and probably by the nuns.

Florence was the most important centre of Italian needlework and it was to this city that the French Dukes of Burgundy and of Berry sent patronage for ecclesiastical items. Few of their vestments have survived but inventories shed some light on imports to France. Florentine needlework was especially related to painting, firstly in design and colouring and secondly the gold backgrounds adopted a form that imitated the gilt gesso backgrounds of panel pictures. The patterns were achieved by first couching down string and then superimposing gold thread. Superbly executed silkwork figures stood out against these with extreme delicacy and with a statuesque serenity similar to that mastered by Florentine painters. A fine altar frontal, signed and dated by its maker, Jacopo Cambi, 1336, displays these qualities clearly. It depicts the coronation of the Virgin by Christ surrounded by groups of angel musicians and further flanked by fourteen saints in pointed Gothic niches. A smaller band above depicts in minute and colourful detail a number of scenes from the life of Christ and the Virgin. This and another Florentine altar frontal are very well preserved.

Sicily had a history of sumptuous silk embroidery, especially in the 12th century. The Royal workshops at Palermo made fine ecclesiastical and court robes including the famous pluvial now in Vienna (*Plate 8a*). In the form of an ecclesiastical cope and considerably inspired by Arab embroiderers, it was made for Roger II's coronation in 1130 and was later used for the coronation rites of the Holy Roman Emperors. The animal motif (in this case a lion overcoming a camel) in dual symmetrical form is closely related to similar stylised pairs in Middle East art. This heraldic image came to Sicily through Byzantium. The outside border of the cloak is worked in beautiful Arabic script, the execution being limited to the use of gold on red silk in a strikingly bold way.[3]

Following the French occupation of the island in 1266 and the massacre of them in the Sicilian Vespers in 1282, many craftsmen fled to Italy, thereby boosting the already growing silk industries of Lucca, Pisa and Venice, but virtually ending the long needlework tradition of Palermo.

Another important set of mediaeval vestments of a later period, the mid-15th century, is that of the Order of the Golden Fleece. Probably made in Brussels, they reflect the influence of several painters and consist of three copes, two dalmatics, a chasuble and two altar antependia (a dossal and an altar frontal). They are enriched with jewels and seed pearls and are still in excellent condition.[4] They were made for the court

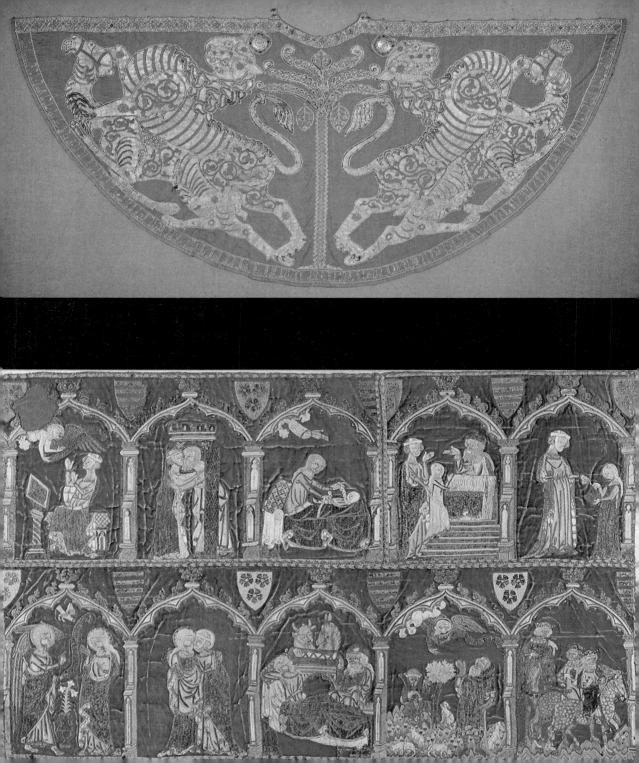

Figure 20
Cope of black velvet
applied with the arms and
fire steel device of the
Duke of Burgundy.
Southern Netherlands
*c.*1475.

Plate 8a (top)
Pluvial or Coronation
Mantle of the Holy
Roman Emperors,
thought to have been
made for Roger II of
Sicily, Palermo, *c.*1130.

Plate 8b (bottom)
Early 14th-century
English bands of red
velvet embroidered with
coloured silks, silver and
silver-gilt threads.

Figure 21
Spanish altar frontal with
sculptural depiction of
St George. Barcelona
*c.*1460.

of the Duke of Burgundy, as were three other surviving cloaks of mourning black silk decorated with heraldry and the Duke's fire steel symbol, from which emanate glistening waves of sparks.[5]

In mediaeval Spain the influence of Moorish work is immediately noticeable in the styles adopted from other parts of Europe. Barcelona was the centre of professional workshops but other towns, notably Toledo and Seville, produced good work. Gold backgrounds were here again a prominent feature, either worked in lines around the design or interlaced, with a trellis effect.

Portugal is especially remembered for a legendary set of robes sent to the Pope by the immensely rich Emanuel, 'lord of the conquest, navigation and commerce of India, Ethiopia, Arabia and Persia' in about 1500. Worked on a gold brocade background, a pomegranate design of real gold had rubies and pearls for seeds and flowers, together with other gems. They must have been dazzling in richness even if somewhat heavy and cumbersome.

It should be recorded that Viking and Celtic settlers in Iceland carried out fine, sophisticated work up to the middle of the 16th century. Local materials rather than silks and velvets were usually the basis for a variety

Figure 22
Part of an altar frontal,
*c.*1540. Ralph Nevill, 4th
Earl of Westmorland,
and his seven sons.

of techniques of couching, appliqué and pattern darning amongst others.

The University of Cambridge, Dunstable Priory and seven of the City of London livery companies[6] have funeral palls of the late 15th and early 16th centuries. The Saddlers' Company has one of crimson velvet with applied embroidery, first worked on pieces of linen, depicting angels, the sacred monogram IHS and the arms of the Company. The Fishmongers', of the late 15th century, shows St Peter enthroned (he is the patron saint of fishermen) with angels, and also St Peter receiving the keys from Our Lord. The Vintners' is of Italian velvet and cloth of gold, embroidered with St Martin of Tours. Rows of kneeling figures, with a discrepancy in size usually denoting status, are a familiar feature of palls and a convention also seen on monuments and church brasses. Many churches had funeral palls; St Margaret's, Westminster, charged a fee of 8d for the use of theirs.

An unusual remnant of the 16th century is the embroidered badge of the Pilgrimage of Grace, 1536–7. It has an emblematic shield and is preserved at Arundel Castle, Sussex. Another needlework banner can be seen in the National Museum of Antiquities in Scotland, a rare survival in that country which suffered so much iconoclasm. Of about 1520 and known as the Fetternear banner, it is thought to be Flemish on

Figure 23
The centre part of the
Fetternear banner,
Flemish *c.*1520.

account of its symbolism. It depicts Christ, pierced and blood-flecked at the foot of the cross and surrounded by instruments used at the crucifixion, together with the cock perched on a pillar. It was never completed and not having been used it is in very good condition.

Mediaeval characteristics gradually gave way to Renaissance ideas, discussed in the next chapter. There is no clear dividing line and combined features can be seen especially in needlework from mainland Europe. The St George altar cloth by Antoni Sadurni of about 1460 preserved at the Chapel of St George in the Palace of the Generalitat, Barcelona, depicts centrally a complex mediaeval rendering of St George with the maiden and the dragon but this is flanked by symmetrical, stylized panels typical of Renaissance ornament, with Italianate gryphons and shields. (*Fig. 21*).

The Reformation prevented a full development of English ecclesiastical needlework in the Renaissance mode. It was the turn of other countries to make the finest vestments. Superb examples of 1554 are at Averbode Abbey, Brabant. These have deep orphrey bands decorated with formalised scrolling foliage, grotesque masks, flowers and fruit, around large roundels depicting narrative subjects in superbly worked detail. But even in the Southern Netherlands where these were made, the production of fine needlework soon declined, largely due to religious persecution, which forced many craftsmen to leave the country.

SECULAR EMBROIDERY

Mediaeval secular embroidery was as great in quantity as ecclesiastical. Although perhaps it never reached the artistic intensity of *opus anglicanum*, it was extravagant in the use of materials and extremely rich and colourful. Even the Squire who went on the Canterbury pilgrimage was attired in needlework according to Chaucer:

> Embrouded was he, as it were a mede
> Al ful of freshe floures whyte and rede.

The royal and princely courts of Europe impressed each other and their subjects with luxurious costumes emphasising their power. Hardly any of these have survived, partly because the garments were not subject to careful veneration as were church vestments. Instead they were continuously used, altered, worn out, taken apart and remade. Another aspect of the secular demands on embroiderers was the making of banners, tunics and horse trappings required for tournaments and ceremonial occasions. But as fashions and customs changed, both costumes and these decorations were allowed to perish. We can only get an impression from illuminations in manuscripts, paintings and written records.

Some early heraldic needlework has survived, however, as on a charter bag of Edward I's reign, at Westminster Abbey. The arms of

Figure 24
Renaissance cope with roundels depicting scenes from the life of St Matthew. Southern Netherlands 1554.

23

England, 'three lions passant gardant, or' are embroidered on a red shield against a green cloth background. The City of London has two other charter bags from the reign of Edward II, dated 1319.

The great seals of Edward I, Edward II and Edward III show on them the elaborate horse trappings used by mediaeval monarchs. Another illustration is to be seen in a stone carving on the tomb of Edmund Crouchback, Earl of Lancaster, son of Henry III, in Westminster Abbey. He died in 1296.

The Black Prince's jupon, a military coat embroidered with his arms, is a fascinating relic preserved by his tomb at Canterbury Cathedral. The quarterings are embroidered on red and blue velvet.

An act of 1364 forbade anybody below a certain income to wear bejewelled costumes and others below another sum to wear any embroidery. But Richard II's court was particularly extravagant with precious garments laden with jewels. As a young man the King himself is said to have had a coat valued at thirty thousand marks. In the Wilton Diptych he is portrayed wearing a rich robe similar to one described in his inventories. When he died in 1399 he left his robes to his servants, after the valuable jewels had been removed. Illustrations of him at the time of his deposition show him dressed in black, embroidered with ostrich feathers—his horse trappings and pennon had the same badge. Robes and hangings were frequently decorated in this manner, 'powdered' with symbols or insignia of suggested, semi-hidden significance. Animals of an heraldic nature were often used. Richard II's most well-known cognisance was a white hart. Queen Philippa, the Black Prince's mother, Richard's grandmother, had a robe decorated with golden squirrels. Further examples can be cited and the tradition lived on until late Tudor times when these *impressas* became even more significant and emblematic.

Charming smaller items of costume to have lasted in greater numbers are alms purses. These were small bags which hung from the belts of rich men and contained such valuables as jewels, money and even relics. They were sometimes elaborately worked with figures and flowers in silks and metal threads. Caen in France was noted for making them.

Other European courts were equally splendid with magnificent needlework. The French dukes of the reigns of Charles V and Charles VI were most lavish and the Dukes of Burgundy and of Orléans were notable patrons of embroidery workshops. There are records of most expensive needlework ordered by Philip the Good, Duke of Burgundy, for his duel in 1425 with Henry Duke of Gloucester at Bruges. A Parisian embroiderer, Tierry de Chastel, was called in to supervise the occasion and many others were summoned from France and the southern Netherlands to carry out impressive decorations. The Duke's personal embroiderer from Bruges, Simon de Brilles, and an artist, Colart de Voleur, were responsible for his tent, banners, tabards and horse trappings. The tent was of blue and white satin and was decorated with the

The great seal of Edward II, and those of many monarchs, shows elaborate embroidered trappings.

24

coats of arms of the Duke's various properties, together with his motto and the Burgundian device of the fire steel and flint.

The French, particularly, loved wall hangings (*salles*), that went round a room in series, and these feature in contemporary documents. In an inventory of Charles V, dated 1364, it is recorded that he had several *salles d'Angleterre* including one of red hangings embroidered with lions, eagles and leopards in blue. These secular embroideries must have been beautiful and, once again, the motifs had heraldic and symbolic nuances. Scrolls with mottos on them, monograms and flowers and animals were sometimes included. Again, the records of the Dukes of Burgundy shed light: Philippe le Hardi, Duke of Burgundy, had hangings of blue satin embroidered with trees by Henriet Goutier of Paris while another of the dukes, Philippe le Bon, had a set of crimson silk hangings with a motif showing a lady bathing a sparrow-hawk.

Bed hangings were especially prized, and impressive beds were a symbol of rank and wealth. They are prominently mentioned in records from mediaeval times until the 18th century as amongst the most important possessions of their owners. Sir John Cobham in 1394 left a bed embroidered with butterflies, and Joan Beauchamp in 1434 one with swans, leopards and flowers. In 1398 John of Gaunt bequeathed his large bed hangings of cloth of gold, embroidered with gold roses and white ostrich feathers, for use on the high altar of St Paul's Cathedral. A little earlier the Black Prince had bequeathed to Canterbury Cathedral a number of embroideries, including wall hangings, several beds and a green velvet robe embroidered with gold for use on the high altar. One bed was embroidered with his arms, another with angels and a third with eagles in blue.

A stranger instance of the conversion of secular needlework to church use is the chasuble now in the Cluny Museum which was almost certainly adapted from horse trappings made for a member of the English royal family. Of superb quality, the pieces are of red velvet, richly embroidered with gold and a little silk. The leopards of England are boldly depicted twice, against a background of small foliage and figures.

Craft guilds strictly supervised the production of needlework. Apprenticeships lasted seven years and in Ghent it was ruled in 1408 that a would-be master had to prove himself on a figure. He also had to have the recommendation of a priest and pay a fee. Old materials could not normally be mixed with new ones and the standard and quality of metal threads was regulated. Work considered below standard was destroyed and sometimes craftsmen were fined. However, the scrutiny was relaxed and gradually standards fell. In 1423 the House of Commons petitioned Henry VI to protect the interests of workshops over the self-employed. The Broderers' Company was subsequently formed in 1430.

Following the Reformation there was a fearful spate of iconoclasm and much of the finest English embroidery was destroyed. Vestments were hacked and burned, metal threads were melted down, and other

Henry VI enthroned. Heraldic needlework has always been a feature of formal state canopies.

valuables were looted from monasteries, convents and churches. It was a sad period but happily some good examples have survived this and later outrages. Even in 1688 an over-zealous Protestant mob, celebrating the Glorious Revolution and the arrival of William and Mary of Orange, raided Traquair in Peebleshire, looting precious ecclesiastical items that had Roman Catholic associations. A description of these includes, '5 vestments . . . one of silk curiously embroidered with gold and silver thread . . . most curiously wrought with a kind of pearl . . . an embroidered eucharist box, two embroidered crucifixes . . .' and ends tersely: 'All solemnly burnt at the Cross at Peebles'.[7]

Many French vestments were lost in the Revolution and were torn, burned and melted down. Perhaps the most sadly missed are a famed set given by René of Anjou to Angers Cathedral. But again, fortunately, there are fine examples to be seen outside France, in Italian and Swedish cathedrals and elsewhere.

Figure 25
Mitre of Archbishop Jean de Marigny, France. Early 14th century.

NOTES

Epigram: Dame Dorothy Selby's tomb at Ightham, Kent, 1641.

1 *Apollo*, July 1972, Philippe Verdier, 'Arts at the Courts of France and England (1259–1328).

2 This fine shape was often used at later periods. *See*, for example, the inlaid decoration on the front of a scriptor with silver mounts, *c*. 1675, in the Duke's Closet, Ham House, Surrey.

3 The use of script as a decorative pattern is an important and beautiful feature of embroidery in the Near and Middle East. Elaborate calligraphy is also seen in Russian needlework.

4 Kunsthistorisches Museum, Vienna. *See also The Connoisseur*, March 1977. Robert L. Wyss, 'The Dukes of Burgundy and the encouragement of textiles in the Netherlands'.

5 Ibid.

6 The Worshipful Companies of Merchant Taylors (2), Fishmongers, Ironmongers, Parish Clerks, Brewers, Saddlers and Vintners. The pall from Dunstable Priory is in the Victoria and Albert Museum.

7 Quoted from a document by Margaret Swain, *Historical Needlework*, 1970.

3 The Post-Mediaeval Period

sapphire, pearl and rich embroidery

IXTEENTH-CENTURY Europe saw great changes in culture and religion. The Renaissance, which had been gathering momentum since its origin in Italy, brought an end to the later mediaeval period, now seen as dark ages, and dispelled elements of mystery and superstition that precluded a more human approach to life. A new spirit of individual thinking led to a cultural revival with a fresh emphasis on personal human philosophies in the fields of learning, science, the arts, and a study of antiquity.

In the meantime, the Reformation caused the Roman Church a substantial loss of spiritual and temporal power and England, becoming independent from Rome, saw increased secularisation in social life. With the House of Tudor firmly established on the English throne, the unrest of the Wars of the Roses was soon forgotten and the country settled down to a period of stability and rapid cultural growth. Literature flowered in the monumental achievements of William Shakespeare and his contemporaries while the decorative arts also reached new standards of remarkable individuality and quality.

Fine church vestments continued to be made in the Catholic countries but significant changes of approach can be noted. Fifteenth-century Italian artists were once again called upon to draw cartoons for embroiderers of copes and other items; a treatise written by Cernino Cennini in 1437 shows that they were now concerned with such technical problems as perspective. The influence of Giotto is notable, with an introduction of naturalism to religious scenes, transcending the hitherto conventional idealistic conception. Figures began to reflect human nature, more subtle than mere symbols of religious passion. Raised, padded work continued to be a feature in the main part of Europe but this was not done in England, perhaps due to an instinctive suspicion of idolatry. In any case, few ecclesiastical pieces were made in this country from the 16th century; these tend to be of a different nature, having personal, secular connotations, like the fine chalice veil in the Burrell collection which is embroidered with the royal arms and an inscription in silk and metal threads.

English needlework had become more domestic in character and largely amateur, rather than professional. In fact, most of the best

pieces surviving from the post mediaeval period onwards are of a secular nature and, furthermore, many were worked by amateurs.

Holinshed, in his *Chronicles* of 1577, mentions that needlework was amongst the chief accomplishments of the women of Elizabeth I's court. This had been the case for some time, for it was considered an essential part of a noble lady's education. It was a privileged pastime, not available to all, since the materials were still relatively scarce and expensive, especially metal threads. The designs were usually drawn out by a man employed for the purpose, and he would often have an eminent place in the household. All ladies of high birth seemed to have enjoyed needlework; they would carry it around with them and do it anywhere, in or out of doors. Catherine of Aragon is said to have had a skein of em-

29

Figure 27
English late 15th or early
16th-century blue velvet
chasuble with applied
orphrey cross, angels,
eagles and rose slips.

broidery silk round her neck when she faced Cardinal Wolsey and Campeggio to answer Henry VIII's accusations.

As a result of Renaissance exploration and trade a new class of successful merchants arose. They emulated the nobility, boasting their riches in a display of luxuries, which included exotic imports from distant countries, extravagant clothes and, in their houses, rich textiles, furnishings and needlework.

Early 16th-century inventories show how secular embroideries and textiles were increasingly fashionable in the greater houses. Hangings for walls and beds, valances, cushions and table carpets are mentioned frequently; all these were often worked by amateurs—the ladies of the household. Linen canvas embroidery in tent stitch was by now the most used technique for household furnishings. On some projects the ladies worked together contributing pieces which were joined or applied to

30

form a whole. Many of the most precious Tudor and Elizabethan embroideries have not survived because they have perished, been eaten by moth, been worn out or been raided for their component materials; much of what has come down to us must be regarded as a relatively humble sample.

The needlework of the Tudor period is curiously divided in its apparent origins of style. In some respects it is clearly related to the Renaissance spirit but in others it is more closely associated with oriental designs. While undoubtedly influenced by Italian, Spanish and Flemish ideas, it was in many ways consciously independent of the continent of Europe, maintaining an individual character. Early Tudor portraits, such as those of Henry VIII (*Plate 9*), show costumes with designs that seem more Eastern than Western; the arabesque patterns are similar to those on garments worn at the Sultan of Turkey's court. This is not altogether surprising since there was considerable interest in that culture and oriental carpets were already popular. These arabesques were usually drawn in the form of strapwork, with a combination of flat bas-relief patterns of bands in lines and arcs interlaced over and under each other. Some aspects of the decoration are attributed to the Moors, coming to England through Spain, and others to Damascus as a by-product of the trading which had been established there. 'Moryshe and Damashin' patterns and the techniques in other fields also no doubt influenced embroiderers. Geometric shapes had certainly been shown in mediaeval designs but now more complex forms were developed in armour, plasterwork, woodwork, pargetting, metalwork, the tooling on leather bookbindings and the lay-out of garden parterres. Strapwork knots in an interlaced link pattern, apparently a world-wide symbol, having been carved on prehistoric stone crosses in ancient Ireland, for example, and still engraved on modern African silver and brasswork, appeared in oriental and Tudor arts.[1] Plain examples were carefully recorded in the earliest surviving English sampler made by Jane Bostock in 1598. Similar designs are common to pattern and instruction books written for both gardening and needlework.

A strapwork knot.

Animal head terminals on strapwork formed the basis of arabesques, and these were carried to a further dimension in 'grotesques'. Supposedly based on 'antique' or classical decoration and derived in name from grottos because they were found underground and excavated, they have strange combinations of linear and animal forms meticulously composed in a light, whimsical vein. They are crowded with flowers, masks, terms and other semi-human forms. Raphael was fascinated by them and inspired others by using them in his decoration of a loggia in the Vatican.

English versions of these formalised patterns were, however, much less complex than the lavish Renaissance decoration carried out by French nobles in their *châteaux*. Francis I, Henri II, his queen, Catherine de Medici, and mistress, Diane de Poitiers, all had fabulously picturesque

castles. Fontainbleau itself was transformed into a glorious palace. Mary Queen of Scots, who spent most of her childhood at the French court, would have been familiar with these places and must have admired the needlework decorations, supplied mostly by professional workshops.

There were still some professional embroiderers in London but their trade had become more specialised and was centred on ceremonial occasions. They undertook preparations for tournaments and provided horse trappings and barge decorations for important events. Much of their work was heraldic; a number of fine seal bags or purses survive, heavily and impressively decorated with the royal arms and cherubs' heads in raised silver thread work. Other commissions included bed valances, table carpets, livery company crowns, bookbindings, gloves and sweet-bags. The last two items especially were amongst traditional gifts and feature several times in lists of presents given to Elizabeth I at the New Year.

The Broderers' Company, a revered institution formed to protect professionals, became somewhat weakened following the Reformation. It grew back to strength, however, and was incorporated under a Royal Charter in 1561. Sadly, its records were lost in the Great Fire in 1666 but it is known that one of its chief duties was to scrutinise all professional work and destroy unfit pieces. The Company also had its own workshops which carried out official and semi-official commissions for pageants, masques, and the Livery Companies. A number of palls, referred to in the previous chapter, still survive, and also Masters' and Wardens' crowns of the Carpenters', Girdlers', Broderers' and Parish Clerks' Companies. The last has a pair dated 1601.

In addition to these responsibilities, it should be remembered that professional embroiderers played an important role in teaching, advising and designing for amateurs all over the country, in England and in Scotland. They travelled widely, preparing and drawing out canvases for amateur needleworkers, frequently assisting in matters akin in design but remote in technique from needlework. Their instruction and guidance was invaluable but did not temper the freshness and originality of amateurs' ideas. On the contrary, many pieces are distinctly and, at times, charmingly, naive.

The favourite subjects worked in Tudor and Elizabethan needlework were flowers, either in sprig form or in continuous scrolling tendril form, country scenes, partly derived from the peasant pictures of Teniers, heraldry, Old Testament stories and tales from Ovid's *Metamorphoses*. Narrative subjects were depicted unashamedly in quaint 16th-century terms. Pattern books, emblem books, allegories and symbols were also drawn upon and a dense scholastic range of idioms was the crux of many designs, as for example in the most famous needlework of the period, the Oxburgh hangings (*Plate 12*). No great changes occurred in the reign of James I, though there was more use of metal threads, spangles and a new emphasis on subjects worked in deep relief.

FLOWERS

Flowers, herbs and plants in general, some of them newly introduced to this country, were of the greatest fascination to 16th-century ladies. They loved them for their beauty and scent, were curious about their medicinal potency, and were amused and charmed by innuendoes of symbolism. They were frequently portrayed in Tudor and Elizabethan decoration, and in literature are constantly placed in a balance between sheer ornament and couched conceit. But they were beloved by needlewomen especially.

In France, Henry IV's embroiderer Jean Vallet was an important figure in court circles. He advised on the botanical gardens in Paris and, in conjunction with Jean Robin, was expected to provide embroiderers with specimen flowers to be used as patterns. These he published in a book of engravings, *Le Jardin du Roi Henri IV* (1608). Similarly, in England there was an intense interest in flowers. Women examined specimens in detail and attempted to record plants with scientific accuracy. The flowers they chose to portray were real ones, but they did not slavishly represent three dimensional groups with dull realism. Each flower or sprig was depicted in 'slip' form with a certain treasured formality. Slips were originally derived from gardeners' cuttings, which were ideal as patterns for small tent stitch pieces, later to be applied to a ground of velvet. Later they were copied from printed herbals. An alternative was to portray real flowers, joined in continuous scrolling patterns, as in the embroidered blackwork on costumes and pillow covers. There would appear to be a connection between this style and the border decorations of illuminated manuscripts where running tendrils of floral patterns also coil regularly and fill the space evenly.

The love of plants, coupled with recording their charm, culminated in the Dutch floral painting of the 17th century and this in turn gave needleworkers further ideas, but the simple, elegant woodcuts that began the floral tradition were particularly appropriate for transposition into needlework. Subject and medium were perfectly suited.

Printing had been invented by Gutenberg in the mid-15th century and soon affected amateur needlework through a greatly increased circulation of ideas and designs. By 1550, several pattern books for needlework were in circulation throughout Europe—Italian and French ones being the first. But books of less direct relevance such as herbals and bestiaries provided considerable inspiration for embroiderers. Lace pattern books suggested certain patterns, and woodcut block illustrations in various works instigated others. The chief sources however began with German woodcuts in *Furm and Modelbuchlein* (1523), while a later book, Jolann Sibmacher's *Schön neues Modelbuch*, published in Nuremberg in 1597, had a wide influence for at least a hundred years. In England Conrad Gesner's *Catalogues Plantarum*, the first principle herbal, was published in 1542 and was the basis of such works as John Gerrard's very popular *Herbal or General History of Plants*, originally printed in 1597 and continuously produced up to 1636. Gardening and embroidery were acknowledged to be closely associated in spirit, and they have always remained so.

Amongst other early flower studies was *La Clef des Champs* by a Hugenot, Jaques le Moyne (London 1586). The dedication in this book indicated that it was intended for all sorts of craftsmen, including embroiderers and tapestry weavers. Some of the illustrations in surviving copies indicate that they were pricked out with pins, for pouncing, a method of tracing the pattern. The book included wild and garden flowers, as well as animals, birds and fruit. Like many illustrated books, it showed a complete disregard of relationships of scale between plants, animals and insects; woodblocks from different sources were juxtaposed with child-like abandon. This scrap-book feature was copied in needlework renderings. Crispin de Passe's *A Garden of Flowers* (1615) was especially useful as a pattern book, the engravings having bold outlines and a formal elegance suited to embroidery, as opposed to being entirely naturalistic. Flowers and fruits are shown in little clumps, often on a small hillock, and with small animals around the bases.[2]

Costume offered wonderful opportunities for fine needlework and was well suited to floral patterns and combinations of small flower portraits. In some respects laborious and magnificent embroidery of this kind replaced the efforts that would earlier have been directed towards church vestments. Such decoration was highly fashionable until the middle of the 17th century when Caroline ladies turned to the

colours, sheen, textures and rustle of plain silks. Queen Elizabeth's wardrobe inventory of 1600 listed, for example, a gown of: 'black satten, embroidered all over with roses and pauncies, and a border of oaken leaves, roses and pauncies, of Venice golde, silver and silke'. Others were decorated with: 'pomegranatts, roses, honiesocles, and acornes'.

Roses were especial favourites, as in every period since. Their intriguing origin in Persia, their relationship with the common briar, their combination of sweet scents with difficult thorny stems, are each aspects of their alluring charm. For Tudor ladies, white and red roses were also the badges of the now united houses of York and Lancaster. The white musk rose with its rambling tendrils was particularly adaptable to pattern making. Carnations, known as gilliflowers, were another favourite and continued to be used in more or less stylised forms well into the 18th century, when all flowers were again treated naturalistically. Pansies, referred to by both Chaucer and Shakespeare as 'love-in-idleness', were very much a hallmark of the 16th century, and frequently carried innuendoes of love. Irises, or *fleurs-de-luce*, peonies, of Chinese origin, and foxgloves, created by Juno when Jupiter threw down her thimble, were amongst other favourites. Also seen were primroses, daffodils, cornflowers, lilies, snowdrops, violets, blue bells, daisies, peascods and marigolds. Honeysuckle was found particularly decorative for its unusually shaped flower and the crawling nature of its growth led to pattern-making and formalised borders. Trees and ferns were depicted but not as often as herbs and fruit. Borage, rue, rosemary, lavender, thyme and germander were delineated in Thomas Tusser's *A Hundreth good pointes of Husbandrie*, first printed in 1561, and became part of the grammar of sewing. A less frequently portrayed newcomer to England was the potato plant, brought from Peru. Raspberries were occasionally embroidered, and strawberries often. Desdemona's problematical handkerchief was 'spotted with strawberries'[3]—these were the wild variety, a symbol of purity. They were brought from the woods, unspoiled by less natural and coarser vegetables grown in the garden. Like the rose, the thistle was of course emblematic, being used sometimes in reference to Scotland or Mary Queen of Scots. It is seen in two pieces at Hardwick Hall, probably cushion covers, worked by Mary, that depict thistles, roses and lilies (for Scotland, England and France) within a net of vine stalks, on a yellow background.

Insects and wild animals also occur frequently, either in tent stitch appliqué pieces 'powdered' over curtains and upholstery, or incorporated in the continuous designs typical of costume. Such creatures were derived from natural history books and pattern books. There was also a great interest in emblems and personal *impressas*, symbols adopted as semi-emblematic badges. Both allusive and illusive, they were part of the colourful language of allegory that was enjoyed for its veiled meanings. The spirit of this acrobatic imagery culminated in the metaphysical poems of John Donne, in which he contrived 'conceits' and 'wit' in much the same manner as was attempted by ingenious amateur needleworkers. The best embroideresses combined elements of Aesop's Fables with devices, mottoes, proverbs, emblems and symbols; indeed the language of Shakespeare, Spenser and Donne is felt throughout their work. Emblem books that were widely influential were Claude Paradin's *Devises Heroiques* (1557, English edition 1591) and Geoffrey Whitney's *A Choice of Emblemes* (1586).

Figure 29
Margaret Laton, portrait attibuted to Marcus Gheeraerts (active 1590–1630).

The portraits of Queen Elizabeth I which are in the National Portrait Gallery, at Hardwick Hall and at Hatfield House show her dressed in magnificently embroidered costumes. Each was a kind of political poster, designed to impress and to convey qualities of the Queen's official character. The dresses are respectively decorated with foliate arabesques in gold thread, flower slips, a combination of flowers, sea creatures and birds, and a collection of emblems. The last of these dresses, in the 'rainbow' portrait at Hatfield, was probably conceived as an idealised, symbolic costume and never existed, but the eyes, ears, serpent and rainbow represented vigilance and sympathy, and these emblems are typical, though extreme examples, of the thinking behind embroidered messages. Symbols such as a rainbow for peace, a compass for constancy and a garland or olive branch for victory were immediately recognisable, while others were tentatively suggestive of equivocal characteristics. Elizabeth's portrait painters were required to paint her in flattering terms for propaganda purposes, but on the whole artists portrayed the wonders of their sitters' costumes with great accuracy. A portrait of Margaret Laton displayed today alongside her bodice in the Victoria and Albert Museum is stunning testimony to the true representation that was customary.

COSTUME EMBROIDERY

Tudor and Elizabethan portraits indeed show magnificent stitchery which has never since been equalled on costume. Precision work and attention to detail contributed to a jewel-like style, displaying a superb, shimmering richness. Very ornate mixtures of patterns were embroidered on every available space, frequently high-lighted with jewels. Even underwear was finely embroidered and the overall costume effect was augmented by accessories, including lace ruffs, feathers in hats, rosettes on shoes, and often a fine lawn or gauze veil worn over embroidered garments. Monarchs naturally had to outshine their courtiers. In 1517 it was recorded that almost 450 ounces of fine gold and 850 pearls were removed from the robes of Henry VIII for re-use. When Elizabeth I died at the age of 70 she left over a thousand dresses heavy with bullion, jewels and gimps. Mary Queen of Scots' inventories are full of interesting detailed lists of her embroidered clothing such as: *Une robbe de satin bleu faicte a borletz toute couverte de broderye en fasson de rosse et feullages faictz*

Figure 30
Margaret Laton's jacket
depicted acurately in her
portrait. Early 17th
century.

37

dargent, et le reste cordonne dor et bordee dung passement dor.[4] This was almost certainly professional work. Most amateur embroidery was done on smaller articles of which there was a great variety. They included jackets, waistcoats, coifs, bonnets, men's caps, hoods, sleeves, stomachers, partlets, gloves, scarves and handkerchiefs as well as smaller carried items like sweet-bags and bookbindings. Reticella and needle-point lace collars, cuffs and fringes provided a contrast to colour, though no less elaborate.

BLACKWORK

Lighter garments were embroidered neatly with blackwork, otherwise known as Spanish work. This monochrome needlework, often but not always done in black, was originally thought to have been introduced to England by Catherine of Aragon but, in fact, the technique was known here before her arrival. Its Moorish qualities are clear in strap-work designs but these are contrasted with curvilinear vine tendrils on both costume and household furnishings, such as pillow covers. A portrait by Gower of Mary Cornwallis (*Fig. 32*) shows magnificent black-work of both forms[5] and one of Elizabeth I at Hever Castle, Kent, shows that even this light work was sometimes enriched with jewels.

Blackwork is especially associated with Henry VIII and his children. Holbein's portraits of them have led to the characteristic double-running stitch technique being termed Holbein stitch. Ruffs and cuffs called for very tidy workmanship with equal neatness on both sides of the material since both sides of the wavy frill showed. Simpler designs were worked on less prominent garments. An example is Dorothy Wadham's shirt which is at the Oxford college founded in her name. In this case narrow diagonal strips are embroidered with vine leaves in purple thread, an unusual colour. Red was sometimes used (as on a jacket in the Victoria and Albert Museum) but black was the most frequent, perhaps reflecting the printer's ink of woodcut illustrations. Patterns were occasionally geometric, even with something like a repeated starfish design and sometimes the embroidery was highlighted with gold or silver thread. Always incorporating real flowers and fruit, scrolling patterns were worked on caps, purses and pillow covers (known then as pillow beres).

Caps or 'coifs' had been worn throughout the Middle Ages but were elaborately embroidered in the 16th and early 17th centuries (*Plate 10a*). Elizabethan ones had a turned up brim around them, others were close-fitting and simple in shape. They were not for night wear, but were used on semi-formal occasions when a wig was not worn and were even sometimes depicted being proudly worn by distinguished men in their portraits. At Audley End, Essex and Trinity College, Cambridge there are portraits of Thomas Neville wearing a splendid cap. Sir Walter Raleigh purportedly wore one under his hat at his execution. Women's coifs were hood-shaped and were sometimes accompanied by a 'forehead cloth' similarly embroidered, and occasionally worn at the same time. These were also worn on domestic occasions such as bed receptions and might be of blackwork, perhaps enriched with silver or gold thread, or alternatively of colourful silks. They were sometimes scented with the perfumes of various flowers, particularly lavender, which was believed to have medicinal qualities. William Turner wrote in his *Newe Herball* (1551) of spikes of lavender: 'quilted in a cap and dayly worne they are good for all diseases of the head that do come of a cold cause and they comfort the braine very well'.

The infilling patterns on blackwork vine leaves were often varied, with contrasting textures reminiscent of, and probably influenced by, needlepoint lace. This feature and the flowing tendril forms of blackwork developed in the 17th century into the greatly expanded crewelwork designs that became so fashionable and were so uniquely English. Contemporary with the fashion for blackwork and following it was the practice of working similar designs much more richly with brighter materials. Coiling stems were frequently worked in gold, linking and enclosing flowers, insects and creatures of brightly coloured silks, while backgrounds were 'powdered' with jewels, pearls and sequins. Gloves of this nature were a status symbol, and were often official gifts. They were usually made professionally and provided a regular trade for a number of craftsmen, culminating in 1638 in the formation of the Glovers' Company under Royal Charter. Elizabethan gloves were of thin tight-fitting leather, doeskin or kid, with gauntlets of embroidered silk with scallop-shaped edges fringed with gold lace. They were often scented. In earlier times a symbol of combat challenge, they were now given formally in presentation ceremonies as a mark of honour, or simply as presents. Sir Thomas More, Chancellor to Henry VIII, was given a pair filled with angels (coins) as a New Year's gift by an admiring and grateful plaintiff, and Queen Elizabeth I was often the recipient of gloves, as on the occasion of her visit to Cambridge University in 1578:

> Also with the book the said Vice-chancellour presented a paire of gloves, perfumed and garnished with embroiderie and goldsmithe's wourke, price 60s. . . . In taking the book and the gloves, it fortuned that the paper in which the gloves were folded to open; and hir Majestie behoulding the beautie of the said gloves, as in great admiration, and in token of hir thankfull acceptation of the same, held up one of hir hands. And when the Oracon was ended, she rendryed, and gave most heartie thanks, promiseing to be mindful of the Universitie.

A pair of gloves in the Ashmolean Museum, Oxford were reputedly left behind to mark the Queen's visit to that university in 1566.

The Elizabethan custom of giving New Year's gifts, especially to the sovereign, must have stimulated much needlework. It was known that

Figure 31
Thomas Neville, Master of Trinity College, Cambridge 1593–1615, portrayed wearing an embroidered cap.

39

the Queen was fond of it and many embroidered items were amongst
the presents that were traditional from all of position and rank, in
church and state. Many of the gifts were subsequently given away as
return presents; in other cases pieces of silver gilt were given. Gifts to
Elizabeth included money, jewels and clothes. Frequently small purses
otherwise known as sweet-bags, were given. Measuring about 4 in x 3 in
(10 cm x 7.6 cm), they were finely embroidered with metal and silk
threads, having drawstrings and tassels of silk. In 1561, the Earl of
Derby gave the Queen a New Year gift of twenty pounds 'in a purse of
cypresse satten, embrawdered with gold, in demy sovereynys'. Scarves
were among other gifts that she received, also books in embroidered
bindings.

Figure 33
Late 16th-century man's
cap decorated with
rainbows, clouds, snails
and other insects.

BOOKBINDINGS

Tudor and Stuart bookbindings were a fascinating though short-lived
phenomenon. A good many have survived so they must have been
numerous. They are mostly small, formal in design, often the work
of professionals, and with one exception the embroidery bears no
reference to the actual book inside. Most were worked on crimson
velvet though isolated cases of other colours and materials are known.
The royal monograms H, HR and ER with insignia such as Tudor roses
and coats of arms are the most usual form of decoration, beautifully
laid out and executed, sometimes with seed pearls in addition to metal
threads. A very beautiful example in this category, in the Bodleian
Library, Oxford, is a Bible which the printer Christopher Barker had
bound in an embroidered binding in 1583 for presentation to Elizabeth I.
Metal threads and seed pearls form a delightful composition of Tudor
roses linked by stylised stems, leaves and birds. Another binding in the

same library containing the Epistles of St Paul is said to have been worked by the Queen herself, when princess, and been given by her to her stepmother Katherine Parr, in 1544. Silver threads are worked in this case on a blue silk background. A book printed in the same, year Petrach's *Opere Volgari*, was given an embroidered binding by Katherine Parr herself. She worked her own complex coat of arms on linen and applied this to purple velvet. It was no doubt a rare work for her since she is alleged to have stated 'My hands are ordained to touch crowns and sceptres, not needles and spindles'. A psalter presented to Queen Mary in 1553, the year in which she became Queen, and now in the British Museum, is decorated with a large flower on each side, reminiscent of ecclesiastical needlework.

Archbishop Parker's *De Antiquitate Britannicae Ecclesiae* (1572) was the first privately printed book in England and a presentation copy was given to Elizabeth I, with an embroidered binding. This has the exceptional feature of alluding in punning fashion to the author in that it depicts a park fence with trees and deer within.

Bookbindings, too, were often scented, perhaps partly to disguise a smell of glue. But when Elizabeth visited Cambridge the Vice-Chancellor was particularly warned that the New Testament bound in red velvet embroidered with the Queen's arms should have no 'savour of spike' (i.e. lavender). The records have not disclosed why.

SAMPLERS

There is evidence in records and inventories to show that samplers were worked extensively in the 16th century. These take their name from the French *essamplaire* and Latin *exemplarium* meaning example, and consisted of small lengths of cloth on which were recorded examples of stitches, border patterns and motifs (*Plates 15 & 16*). Originally they were limited to the specific function of being a kind of notebook which was always at hand, embroidered with snippets of model techniques and designs for adapting to costume decoration. These were jotted down at random, usually by adults, but by the 17th century they began to be regarded as exercises in mastering techniques and designs for young children, in addition to being private collections for continuous reference. In the 18th century, they were looked upon as achievements in themselves to be admired as diminutive works of art. Instead of being kept rolled up in the sewing box, they were framed and hung on parlour walls.

Samplers are mentioned several times in Elizabethan literature, notably by Skelton and Sir Philip Sidney, while Shakespeare indicates how girls were so involved in sewing them that they became useless in conversation:

Fair Philomel, she but lost her tongue,
And in a tedious Sampler sewed her mind.[6]

Plate 10a (top)
A blackwork coif or headress (opened out) with a leaf and berry design and enriched with gilt spangles. Late 16th century.

Plate 10b (bottom)
Part of one of a set of Elizabethan pillow covers in pristine condition. A variety of flowers are embroidered in silk and the background is of gold thread.

Barnabe Riche, in his story *Of Phylotus and Emilia* (1581), relates how Emilia will live in comfortably rich circumstances when married and will go about various activities including the use of her samplers in the way they were originally intended.

> Now, when she had dined, then she might seke out her examplers, and to peruse whiche worke would doe beste in a ruffe, whiche in a gorget, whiche in a sleeve, which in a quaife, which in a caule, whiche in a handkercheef; what lace would doe beste to edge it, what seame, what stitche, what cutte, what garde: and to sitte her doune and take it forthe by little and little, and thus with her nedle to passe the after noone with devising of thinges for her owne wearynge.

The earliest reference to an actual sampler is in an account book of Queen Elizabeth of York[7] of 1502 where there is an entry: 'an elne of linnyn cloth for a sampler for the Queene, viijd.' There are other references to samplers of both coloured threads and plain white cut and drawn work, but the first indicating the purpose of a sampler is in Edward VI's inventory of 1552 where there is a record of 'a sampler or set of patterns worked on Normandy canvas with green and black silks'.

A fine, whitework Tudor sampler in the London Museum is in the traditional form of a long thin band worked with many rows of embroidery and lace patterns across the narrow width, including the royal arms. One row is worked in gold thread and another in silver; the use of coloured silks incorporated in such pieces is very rare.

Though no early ones have survived there must have been a practice too of making polychrome samplers in non-whitework techniques. These were, as already stated, made in preparation for the embroidery of dresses; designs included arabesques, natural history motifs and emblems, in addition to a variety of border patterns and other motifs.

Figure 34
Small purse and pincushion in coloured silks and with a background of silver thread. Early 17th century.

DOMESTIC FURNISHINGS

Renaissance liberalism and increased trading brought to the 16th-century nobility a desire and taste for greater comfort and luxury. Fine materials had become more accessible and the emphasis of workmanship that had been directed to church use was now available for secular patronage. Professional embroiderers were employed to a considerable extent on the provision of furnishings for important houses. In England a great part, perhaps the larger part of the needlework done for domestic use, was carried out by the enthusiastic amateurs of the household. Bess of Hardwick's great new mansion, Hardwick Hall, for instance, was remarkable for its needlework furnishings; many of these appear to have been worked by Bess herself, her friends, companions and staff. She was undoubtedly guided by professional draughtsmen, but the actual sewing was usually the much enjoyed and envied pursuit of the privileged ladies who had the time to do it.

Amongst the quantities of textiles that became so popular and made houses less draughty and more comfortable were, in addition to imported tapestries and oriental carpets, needlework and appliqué hangings for walls and for large four poster beds, and also table carpets, cushions, pillow covers and smaller items. Two very fine petit point hangings at Scone Palace, Perth, are in a form more familiar in tapestry weaving, and must have been made by professionals. The larger one depicts, within a complex border of symbolic figures, animals and putti, Justice and Mercy embracing. They are supported and crowned by putti and the landscape background incorporates religious and pastoral scenes. Needlework carpets were made in both England and in continental Europe with designs closely imitating Turkish knotted ones. Interlocking geometric strapwork formed the basis of the patterns and included a modification of the Eastern Cufic pattern.[8] These should not be confused with 'turkeywork' imitations of oriental carpets made by knotting, which enjoyed great popularity and were also used for upholstering furniture. A set of twelve cushions of this technique, ten of which are now in Norwich Cathedral, were made for the use of the aldermen when using Blackfriars Hall in Norwich. Carpets of this type and needlework ones in an oriental style, and true oriental rugs were used simultaneously; indeed the 1601 inventory of Hardwick Hall shows that these, needlework carpets and more conventional European forms were interchangeable: 'a long table of white wood, a fayre Turkie carpet for the same table, an other fayre long carpet for it of silk nedlework with gold frenge lyned with crimson taffetie sarcenet. . .'.

English carpets were often elaborate in design and are so perfect that it is likely that many were made professionally. The designs of surviving examples have complex overall patterns lacking the naivety which one would expect to see in amateur work. Two carpets in the Victoria and Albert Museum illustrative of this are the Gifford table carpet of about 1550, and the Bradford table carpet of a few decades later. Both are worked in silk tent stitch on canvas. The first has small geometric patterns overall with three large medallions. One of these contains the Gifford arms, the other two have vignettes showing a stag sitting under an oak tree. Each medallion is framed by a wreath of flowers. The Bradford carpet has a large main panel of trellis over which are tightly wound tendrils of vine, heavily laden with grapes, arranged in a stiff formalised pattern, in the Renaissance tradition. Around this there is a border depicting, in superb detail, scenes of rural life on hillocky ground. Hunters, shepherds, fishermen and gentry with many domestic and wild animals are seen with a variety of castles, farmsteads, mills and bridges. All are full of life and portrayed with wonderful workmanship. Since there are no signs of naivety and as the pattern is repeated on both sides of the carpet, it seems the more certain that it was made by professional embroiderers. The plainer patterned parts of both carpets would have

been exceedingly tedious for an amateur to have sewn.

Another entry in the Hardwick inventory notes a carpet: 'of nedle-worke of the story of David & Saul with a golde frenge & trymmed with blew taffetie sarcenet . . .' This may have been of the densely crowded courtly style supposedly introduced from France by Mary Queen of Scots. Close to tapestry in design, this type of needlework is seen on bed valances, table carpets and cushions. Large figures in classical and religious scenes are portrayed in the full courtly costume of 16th-century France. Another carpet in the Victoria and Albert Museum, of this style, shows an extraordinary group of courtiers playing the story of Lucretia's Banquet. Around them are small sections containing fruit trees, a unicorn, birds, dogs and other animals, within broad strapwork divisions. There are curious Tudor heads in the four corners supporting plumes of feathers, an 'Indian' device. Several other similar items exist; some may have been made in France.

Cushions were another symbol of prosperity and luxury. Listed as 'cushyns', 'cosshens', 'quitions' etc., they occur frequently in inventories and records. Though quite large in size, they were less ambitious exercises in needlework and more manageable. The underside was never worked but was 'lined' with plain material. They softened hard furniture and were scattered about the best rooms. It was considered a status symbol to have them; even 'a fair large cushion made of a cope or altar cloth'[9] was worth remarking on.

Figure 35
Detail of the Bradford table carpet showing sections of the border and central panel. Late 16th-century.

Professional embroiderers were commissioned to make for the Ironmongers' Company, in 1563, twelve cushions 'with the company's arms wrought in every of them' but, on the whole, surviving examples appear to be of amateur workmanship. They can be divided into roughly seven varieties. Firstly, there were large oblong tent stitch cushions depicting allegorical or mythological subjects, others with courtly-costumed figures, and others with armorial devices sometimes surrounded by stylised foliage. There are good examples of each kind at Hardwick Hall. There were also cushions of velvet decorated with applied embroidered slips, and cushions with raised embroidery including metal threads, depicting insects, animals and flowers. Finally, there were mourning cushions, as listed amongst the possessions of the Earl of Shrewsbury at Sheffield Castle, as well as a humbler sort of woollen cushion, examples of which are at Chasleton House, Gloucestershire. Occasionally topical events were embroidered. A panel, probably for a cushion, in the Lady Lever Art Gallery commemorates a safe deliverance following the Armada and the Gunpowder plot. As a young girl, Elizabeth I made a cushion for her governess in silk and wool, in tent and cross stitches and in 1598 Paul Hentzner, a splendid recorder of his travels, noted seeing at Windsor Castle a cushion 'most curiously wrought by Elizabeth's own hand'.[10] A charming cushion in Cogenhoe Church, Northamptonshire, of about 1600, depicts flower slips within an interlacing knot pattern, with a red scale pattern border. (*Fig. 117*).

Hentzner also mentions the magnificent state beds of Edward VI, Henry VII and Henry VIII at Windsor which he says were each eleven foot square and had brilliant gold and silver quilts. Mediaeval manuscripts and early paintings show how important fine beds were and what efforts were made to make them splendid; their frequent inclusion in illustrations indicates how much they were treasured. In the 16th century new energies were directed towards fine bed hangings, bed coverlets and pillow covers (known then as pillow beres).

There were three principal types of needlework bed hangings. No complete sets have survived since they were exposed to dirt and heavy use. Valances have tended to last better due to the fact that they were non-moving parts and were not subjected to continual handling. These were of a type, similar in style to the carpets and cushions mentioned above, that display narrative scenes with courtly figures. (*Plate 11a*) Originally thought to be French, they are more likely to be professional work made in Scotland, in Perth or in Edinburgh. Of complex design and workmanship in tent stitch, they are visually busy, showing elaborately costumed people packed closely together. The costumes were thought to be French, so the tradition grew that the hangings were brought from France by Mary Queen of Scots. But since the styles appear to postdate Mary's arrival in Scotland, it is more likely that they were of Scottish manufacture of the 1580s and 1590s, perhaps in a French tradition. One piece is dated 1594. The valances were ideal for a narrative sequence of events often being based on engravings of classical stories or Bible illustrations, especially ones by Bernard Salomon and from *Antiquitates Judaicae*, (Frankfurt, 1580) and *Thesaurus Sacrarum*, (Antwerp, 1585). These were curiously transposed into elaborate modern dress depicted in minute detail. Additional small scenes in the background or foreground show interesting views of gardens and domestic furnishings. *Figs 37 & 38* show a less formal example.

The second type of bed hanging is represented by a curtain in the

Figure 37
Jacob at the well, a panel, dated 1594, part of the same set of valances as the one illustrated in *Fig. 38*.

48

Figure 38
One of a set of bed
valances showing scenes
of the story of Jacob and
Esau. Companion valance
dated 1594.

Royal Scottish Museum, Edinburgh, from Linlithgow Palace. This is of a red woollen material appliquéd with large formalised plants, small heraldic lions and borders, each worked in yellow silks on black velvet. They are very striking, and survivals of this kind are rare.[11]

The third type was more numerous. These were of amateur workmanship, closely related to the floral needlework discussed earlier. Based on woodcuts, the motifs on them included flowers especially, but also animals, heraldry and biblical subjects, each with naive charm and spontaneity. Sometimes many hundreds of small pieces were applied to velvet curtains and to make these as many sewers as possible were gathered together. Bess of Hardwick wrote in 1585 that she had called upon all sorts of her staff to assist: 'grooms, women and some boys she kept wrought the most part of them'. A number of embroidered flower pieces and insects made by the Fitzwilliam family have survived at Milton, near Peterborough, being preserved in folios dated 1587–93, while at Glamis Castle, Angus, there are magnificent blue linen hangings applied in the late 17th century with slips worked about one hundred years earlier. Mary Queen of Scots is said to have been associated with the bed hangings of Scone Palace and Florentine ones at Parham Park, Sussex; she certainly undertook magnificent needlework hangings of a different nature now at Oxburgh Hall, Norfolk, to be discussed shortly.

Some beds had 'paned' hangings, that is curtains of joined panels of material, with contrasting colours or textures. They might be of plain silk, damask, velvet or needlework.

Pillow covers were extensively made for use in bedrooms. They were often embroidered with blackwork vine or floral patterns on linen.

Another form of hanging was made of applied materials. These were used more for wall decoration than for beds, and perhaps for screening. They are well represented by a fascinating set of five at Hardwick, one of which is dated 1573. They were probably made by professionals on account of their large scale, these being twelve feet high. A wide variety of rich fabrics was used, including pieces of velvet damask and cloth of gold taken from old vestments. The hangings depict the Virtues and figures representing qualities and opposite 'vices' such as Hope and Judas, Faith and Muhammed. The Virtues—Magnanimity and Prudence, Constancy and Piety, Fortitude and Justice, Chastity and Liberality—are depicted with the characters of Zenobia, Penelope, Cleopatra and

49

Lucretia illustrating them. Personified sciences are also shown, under arches—Grammatica, Rhetorica, Arithmetique, Architecture, Perspective and Astrologie.

MARY QUEEN OF SCOTS

Continuously buffeted during most of her life by political and religious dispute, and always weighed on a curious balance of admiration and threat in the eyes of her cousin Queen Elizabeth, Mary Stuart, Queen of Scots, was also a remarkable figure in the history of needlework. She became devoted to it in childhood and practised it up to the day of her execution, at the age of forty-four.

The daughter of James V of Scotland and Marie de Guise (also known as Mary of Lorraine), Mary was born in 1542 and on the death of her father only six days later, became Queen of Scots. At the age of six years, she was sent to France where she was brought up in the court of the French King, Henry II, and was pronounced Queen of England by the Catholic world which considered Elizabeth illegitimate. At sixteen she was married to the Dauphin Francis, and in the following year they became King and Queen of France. Following Francis's death eighteen months later, Mary returned to Scotland in 1561 and from that moment was at the centre of controversy, loved by many but suspected by others. Political plots and stormy relationships tried the loyalty of her nobles and caused her to be subjected to miserable periods of doubt and anti-Catholic feeling. Only six years after her return to Scotland she was taken prisoner and subsequently spent the last twenty years of her life in custody in Scotland and in England. But throughout her troubled reign, Mary took solace in her embroideries. Roy Strong was not exaggerating when he wrote charmingly of them as: 'silent letters to posterity in handwriting of rainbow silks and metallic thread telling of the misfortunes of a martyred Queen'.[12] They demonstrate her sadness in terms of allegory and symbol. It would have been too dangerous to express her thoughts in words. Needlework of this nature was on a bed which the Queen left to her son James VI of Scotland and James I of England, and in the Oxburgh hangings (*Plate 12*). The bed was decorated with *impressas*, heraldic and proverbial, and with Latin and Italian tags in similar vein, or anagrammatic. Many are sad, as recorded in detail by William Drummond of Hawthornden in a letter to Ben Jonson: '. . . An embleme of a Lyon taken in a Net, and Hares wantonly passing over him . . .' and '. . . A vine tree watred with Wine, which instead to make it spring and grow, maketh it fade. . .'.

The young Mary Stuart had the benefit of a sound training in needlework at the French court and was no doubt taught with the other princesses by their mother, Catherine de Medici. Queen Catherine was herself an expert, having learned the art at a convent in Florence. She was an especially able worker of lacis (darned net whitework) and when

Plate 11a (top)
Late 16th-century bed valance (detail) showing figures in courtly dress in a landscape, a type of needlework that was introduced to Scotland from France. This panel is traditionally associated with Mary Queen of Scots.

Plate 11b (bottom)
Part of a 17th-century wool hanging in Hungarian or Florentine stitch.

she died in 1589 left nearly a thousand pieces of this work. Wool was bought for Mary Stuart when she was nine for her to 'learn to make works' and no doubt she quickly graduated to silks.

When she returned to Scotland she brought certain French servants with her including an embroiderer, Pierre Oudry, but life was made no more easy for them than it was for the Queen. In 1567 Mary was imprisoned in Lochleven Castle for ten and a half months. It is during this

Monogram of Mary Queen of Scots.

period that she is supposed to have worked the many large pieces which are probably wrongly attributed to her. Certainly she could not have achieved them all; it is unlikely that she had such a calm time, the necessary assistance or the right materials. She had to plead in a letter to the Lords of the Council for an apothecary, a page and 'an imbroiderer to drawe forth such worke as she would be occupied about'. During this unhappy period Mary worked in silks 'little flowers painted in canvas'. These were the sort that were later applied to velvet bed curtains such as examples at Scone Palace.

After escaping from Lochleven, Mary fled to England and in the following year, 1569, she was placed in the custodianship of the Earl of Shrewsbury at Tutbury Castle. This semi-imprisonment satisfied Elizabeth I that the threat of a political uprising was limited but by fortunate chance it led to a great needleworking partnership between Mary and her custodian's wife, Elizabeth Shrewsbury, otherwise known as Bess of Hardwick. Both were passionate embroiderers and stimulated each other, and Mary turned to this as relief from her political fate.

'This Queen continueth daily to resort to my wife's chamber where . . . she useth to sit working with the needle in which she much delighteth and in devising works.'[13] So wrote Lord Shrewsbury to Sir William Cecil, Elizabeth's Secretary of State. At the same time Nicholas White, an envoy, wrote to him reporting a meeting at which he was hospitably received by the Queen, who was seated under a canopy of estate, embroidered with Marie de Guise's motto and *impressa*, a phoenix in flames. He, too, described how Mary occupied herself:

> I asked hir Grace, sence the wether did cutt off all exercises
> abrode, howe she passed the thyme within. She sayd that all
> that day she wrought with her nydill, and that the diversitie of
> the colors made the work seme lesse tedious and contynued so
> long at it till veray payn made hir to give over . . .

Bess of Hardwick, was 22 years older than Mary Queen of Scots but the two women undoubtedly enjoyed each other's company. Bess was ever eager to build new houses and furnish and decorate them magnificently. Certainly she must have learned a great deal from the exiled Queen who had known considerable splendour at the French court and to a degree in Scotland. They did much needlework together including, especially, a remarkable memorial to both of them, the Oxburgh hangings (*Plate 12*).

There were four of these hangings in all, but one has since been cut up. Two of the surviving ones are associated with Bess, the third with Mary. These three are at Oxburgh Hall, Norfolk and the other various pieces are in the Victoria and Albert Museum and at Holyroodhouse, Edinburgh. One hanging is dated 1570. Not necessarily intended for use on a bed, they consist of green velvet curtains with over a hundred variously shaped appliqué panels of tent stitch needlework, linked by a light pattern of red and silver thread. Each hanging has a central symbolic picture surrounded by eight octagonal pieces and up to twenty-eight others in cruciform shape. About thirty pieces are signed with royal or personal monograms of the Queen, and fifteen with Bess's initials, E.S. The designs are derived from several natural history and emblem books, many from Conrad Gesner's *Historia Animalium* (c.1560) and others from sources such as Claude Paradin's *Devises Heroiques* (1557), Whitney's *A Choice of Emblems* (1586) and Gabriel Faerno's *Fables* (1563). But they also include many personal emblematic pictures and devices. Mary's embroiderer, Pierre Oudry, may have drawn the outlines on canvas following and adapting woodcut illustrations. The three central panels are especially allusive: the one on Mary's hanging depicts a hand reaching from the sky with a sickle pruning a vine, between two other fruit trees. A motto, a cipher and the Scottish Royal Arms are also shown. Bess's two main panels show tears falling on quicklime, and a jackdaw drinking from a large vase, alluding respectively to her late husband Sir William Cavendish and the Earl of Shrewsbury. Bess was married four times and her needlework refers repeatedly to her husbands.

The Marian hanging also includes, in octagonal panels, monograms, a crowned palm tree with a tortoise climbing it, and a marigold reaching for the sun, each alluding to Mary's repressed status. Cruciform panels show a phoenix (her mother's *impressa*), a dolphin, a lion, a unicorn and exotics such as 'A Sea Moonke'. This curious fish resembling a tonsured monk with a scaly body, fins and flippers, was supposed to have been washed up on the Dutch coast and to have lived and worked with the local women for some time.

The Oxburgh hangings, of course, are delightful for their great charm as well as being exceptional needlework and historically important. This is the only needlework certainly ascribed to Mary Queen of Scots, apart from the two cushions at Hardwick, already referred to. The green velvet backing may be a later replacement but in essence the hangings convey much of the feeling and mood of the period.

An inventory of the Queen's possessions made at Chartley Hall in 1586, shortly before her execution, lists large quantities of needlework including flower slips, 'birds of different kinds', fish, and 'four footed beasts'. This could well refer to parts of the Oxburgh hangings or may be additional work carried out by, or under, the supervision of Charles Plouvart who was Mary's last embroiderer. He, with her other servants, was eventually dismissed by her captors as unnecessary. Even when the Queen was charged at Chartley and committed for trial she was robbed, not only of her papers and jewels but also of her embroidered doublets, scarves and silk stockings.

Though her son James was under the guardianship of lords hostile to Mary's cause and was subject to their influence, he received from her many letters and gifts. She wrote for him 'all with her own hand' a book of French verses and nearly twenty years later the Bishop of Winchester reported that Mary 'wrought a cover of it with a needle, and is now of his Majestie esteemed as a precious jewel'. Unfortunately this has not survived, but at Arundel Castle, Sussex there are some child's reins with a breast plate said to have been worked by the Queen of Scots for her son. They are decorated with likely symbols—sceptres, a lion, an infant and a heart, each crowned—on red silk in gold and silver threads.

A remarkable number of interesting records of the Queen's possessions and accounts survive; for these we must thank her splendid and loyal servants. Her devoted French chamberlain, Servais de Condé, must be specially remembered for his meticulous lists of furnishings and textiles. Mary's will clearly indicates items to be distributed to friends and servants. Amongst them was: 'furniture for a bed wrought with needlework, of silk, silver and gold, with divers devices and arms, not thoroughly finished . . . to be delivered to the King of Scottes'. This is the bed referred to earlier and described in a letter to Ben Jonson in 1619. Unfortunately, it has not survived. A caged bird watched over by a menacing hawk was another emblem on it and very typical of the embroidered decoration. Mary also left a set of lacis bed hangings, only partially completed. These were to go to Jane Kennedy, one of the two women who accompanied her to the execution block. At Conway Castle

Plate 12
The central part of one of the Oxburgh hangings applied with panels worked by Mary Queen of Scots and Bess of Hardwick.

Figure 39
Corner of a fine linen
tablecloth with squares
of darned net, filet or
lacis derived from
pattern books. Signed
'I.A.C.' and dated 1638.
(8 ft 5 in x 7 ft 3 in).

there is a contemporary example of this darned net work. St Paul's and
Exeter Cathedrals have records of early pieces of lacis, but on the whole
it was more popular on the European continent than in England.

Before leaving this period, it is interesting to note how contemporary
embroidery in other parts of the world was mostly of a very different
nature. By the 16th century, England had developed an individual and
unique style, related in some respects to oriental and European influences, but more often contrasting with embroideries worked abroad.
Spain had strong links with North Africa and Latin America. Portugal
had a similar link with India, as a result of opening up the sea route to
Asia in the previous century. Considerable exchanges of trade were
already in operation. Fine yellow silk embroidery on white cotton was
being imported for the European market from Bengal; large coverlets
were densely covered with chain stitch in natural yellow wild silk (faded
to buff) and in pictorial form incorporating a large range of oriental and
European subjects.[14] This was followed by red and blue work from Goa,
which reached a height of popularity and then died away in the 17th
century. Nothing could have differed more from English emblematic
needlework. Meanwhile, far afield in another direction, in Russia, a
strong tradition of embroidery produced remarkable ecclesiastical work
in the 16th century. Coloured silks were heavily embroidered with couched silver, silver-gilt and gold threads, also with vast quantities of

pearls and jewels, especially rubies and emeralds. A chalice cover made in 1598 in the Tsarine's workshop demonstrates these lustrous features.[15] A bold inscription worked in gold threads is designed so as to form a border; within this saints with flesh parts minutely worked are of the mediaeval tradition, with infinite expression. In Russia great expense and effort was directed to needlework which was ostensibly for church use. In France, England and other neighbouring countries, the emphasis was almost entirely secular and personal, and for worldly luxury. Furthermore, it was known that a great display of magnificent costume, houses and furnishings won political and personal sway. It is not surprising that complaints were sometimes audible, such as those made concerning Catherine de Medici in 1586: 'all the revenues are wasted on embroideries, insertions, trimmings, tassels, fringes, hangings, gimps, needleworks, small chain stitchings, etc., new diversities of which are invented daily'. But the formal nature of French needlework appeared opulent when compared with the more domestic work of English amateurs. Trimmings, tassels, fringes and gimps, however, were soon amongst the novel luxuries perfected in all the palaces and great houses of England and Europe in the 17th century.[16]

NOTES

Epigram: Shakespeare, *The Merry Wives of Windsor*, 5.v.74.

1 The everlasting knot of life pattern is also one of the auspicious symbols of Buddhism, found throughout Asia.

2 George Wingfield Digby, *Elizabethan Embroidery*, 1963, lists pattern books.

3 Shakespeare, *Othello*, 3.iii.442.

4 Inventory of Royal Wardrobe at Holyroodhouse, Edinburgh, February, 1562.

5 A splendid portrait of Captain Thomas Lee by Marcus Gheeraerts, dated 1594, shows him dressed in masque costume, as an Irish Knight with bare legs for walking through bogs. He is however wearing a shirt of elaborate and beautiful blackwork. (Tate Gallery, London).

6 Shakespeare, *Titus Andronicus*, 2.iv.

7 Wife of Henry VII.

8 See examples in Landes Museum, Zurich.

9 Heylin, *History of the Reformation*, 1661.

10 *Travels in England*, 1598.

11 Hangings of a similar technique are at Berkeley Castle, Gloucestershire.

12 Roy Strong, *Mary Queen of Scots*, 1972.

13 Calendar of Scottish Papers II, 632, no. 1020.

14 A magnificent early example with intricately worked European figures and oriental animals is in the Isabella Stewart Gardner Museum, Boston. Another is in the Cooper-Hewitt Museum, New York. *See also* Irwin and Hall *Indian Embroideries*, Calico Museum.

15 Kremlin Museum, Moscow.

16 Macramé fringes had already been established in Italy, being derived from those on Turkish towels, the Turkish word 'macrama' meaning towel.

4 The Seventeenth Century

Rayed with golde, and ryght well cled
In fyne black sattyn doutremere.

HE 17TH CENTURY began with the full flowering of Elizabethan needlework which became increasingly rich, with more use of coloured silks as well as more silver and gold thread. The characteristic lightness of silk blackwork fell slightly out of favour, though its monochrome form was adapted to similar embroidery in wool, leading to crewelwork designs for bed curtains. The jacket decorated with scrolling tendrils of flowers in red at the Victoria and Albert Museum is representative of an intermediary stage in this development.

Elizabethan embroideries, in the meantime, quickly reached a crescendo of bejewelled colour, and fanfares of metallic threads heralded the raised and padded needlework that predominated during James I's reign. A magnificent example of this latter type, perhaps English professional work, is a panel at Compton Wynyates, Warwickshire, showing Orpheus charming the wild animals.[1] Another is a gilt bullion casket at Drayton House, Northamptonshire, with raised flowers and animals worked entirely in seed pearls. Such achievements subsequently gave way to more divergent branches of needlework throughout the century which were subject to strong crazes of fashion. These included sampler making, stumpwork and crewelwork, each highly individual and hardly related. The century ended with a certain self-assured solidness brought about by a happy influx of Dutch ideas which, with French overtones, blended and guided all English craftsmanship.

Throughout the century there was a preponderance of flower ornament, in more complex and varied uses and, by the reign of William and Mary, a noticeably greater quantity of colour. Real flowers gave way at times to stylised forms or exotic oriental varieties.

Fashions did not change dramatically after the accession of James I in 1603. Margaret Laton's bodice of about 1610, as already mentioned, alongside a portrait in which she wears it, (*Figs 29 & 30*) shows this period's embroidery at its best. Curling gold tendrils support numerous flowers, birds and butterflies, with the rhythm and sugary variation of a madrigal. Caps, bags and many other articles were similarly embroidered, frequently with backgrounds of gold or silver threads.

The precision of the designs and the quality of the stitchery suggest that a good deal of this needlework was made professionally. Like the

Figure 40
Early 17th-century small casket of faded green velvet, profusely embroidered with couched gold thread and purl, the raised animals and flowers overlaid with seed pearls and studded with larger pearls and garnets.

many formal New Year gifts given to Elizabeth I, it is probable that some articles were made in workshops for presentation purposes. Sweet bags were frequently given; an inventory of Henry Howard, Earl of Northampton, of 1614 describes no less than seventeen. One was 'embrodered with highe embosted mosse worke having two sea nymphes upon dolphins and other figures of fowles, edged about with lace of silver and gold, lined with carnation'.[2] Others are described as having 'knottes of silver Oes with burning hartes'. These small bags were sometimes accompanied by a tiny tasselled pincushion or heart shaped purse. *See Fig. 34.* The most usual decoration was formalised Tudor roses, and other flowers within curling tendrils, on a metal thread background.

Gloves were another popular gift. Stuart ones were larger than the Elizabethan, with more stylised embroidery that extended on to the glove itself from the gauntlet, which was often zig-zag shaped at the opening and trimmed with gold lace. Deep fringes of white linen lace later became very fashionable.

Another unusual survival is a set of early-17th-century falconer's accoutrements embroidered with musk roses and mistletoe. Consisting of bag, lure, gauntlet glove and three hoods, they were purportedly left by James I at Wroxton Abbey as a souvenir of his visit to Lord Dudley

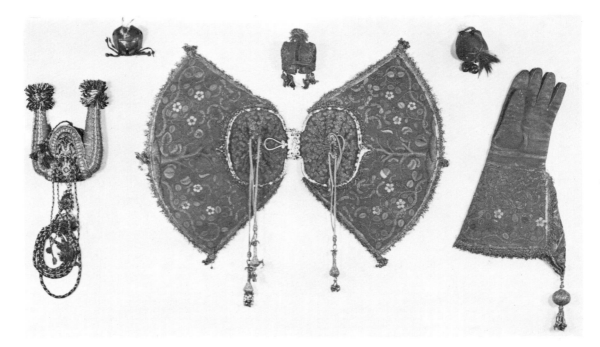

Figure 41
Early 17th-century set of
falconer's accoutrements
given by James I to Lord
Dudley North.

North, and are now in the Burrell Collection.[3] Another fascinating relic,
at Parham Park, Sussex, is a state saddle used by James II on a visit to
Bristol in 1686.

All the foregoing were probably made in professional workshops,
but much was also done by amateurs. Women made sure that their
daughters were studious in discipline and training, to inherit from them
as many skills and stitches as they knew. Girls were increasingly expected
to work samplers to record and practise borders and motifs. From this
they graduated to doing test pieces in pictures, stumpwork, beadwork
or crewelwork. Samplers gradually became removed from practicality
with more elaborate patterns than ever used for costume, and the other
exercises were each looked upon as separate crafts, combining a training
in discipline with practice in sewing and entertainment. Seventeenth-
century stitches were numerous and have evocative names such as
plaited braid, guilloche, Russian overcast, Algerian eye, Montenegrin
cross, Roumanian and double running, to name just a few. They were
combined with rich materials, which were now easier to obtain. Silks
and velvets, even when cut or figured, did not necessarily oust embroidery
but were combined or contrasted with it. A magnificent French bed in
the Louvre from Château d'Effiat is of figured red velvet with elaborate
embroidery. A combination of fine textiles was a feature of professional
workshops and, especially, in the making of church vestments.

Archbishop Laud took office in 1633 and advocated the reintroduction
of High Church traditions. He took steps to re-establish fine needlework,

and some good pieces were made. Two have survived from a set of pulpit and altar hangings commissioned for the Chapel of the Holy Ghost, Basingstoke, by the Sandys family of the Vyne. They are of purple velvet with, respectively, embroidered cherubs' heads with scroll ornament, and the Last Supper. Other ecclesiastical needlework was imported from continental Europe where, following the Counter Reformation, notable work was carried out. In Austria, for example, gold monochrome embroidery was done on bright satin, often red. A shimmering effect was produced with a variety of metal techniques in dramatic stylised patterns. Other good vestments were made in Augsburg where workshops had been influenced largely by Bohemian art, and a fair number of Italian and French ecclesiastical items have survived from the 17th century. A fine set of French vestments, including a cope, a chasuble and two dalmatics, in bright silk chenilles couched on cream damask, from the Carmelite Convent in Darlington, are to be seen at the Bowes Museum, Yorkshire.

By the 1670's, Russia produced some of the finest ecclesiastical needlework, widely derived from Eastern and Western styles. A luxuriously rich cope in the Kremlin is of cut red and green velvet pile on cloth of gold with a border of silver and gold lace on yellow silk. It has a deep collar of emerald green, densely embroidered with pearls and sequins, with a border bearing a long inscription worked in pearls, the lettering being about an inch deep. While this cope shows designs of Islamic influence, a superb coffin cover of 1678 in the same museum displays Russian Orthodox figure embroidery comparable with *opus anglicanum* of 1350. (*Plate 13a*) It is in the traditional form of a Greek Orthodox *epitaphios*. The main panel depicts Christ's prostrate figure, adored by saints and angels, in gloriously varied textures and colours. Our Lord's body and the Virgin's head are outlined in pearls, and the gold thread parts are worked in various geometric patterns. A deep border shows half figures of saints in interlocked roundels on a green silk background. Again, inscriptions are worked into the embroidery as an integral part of the decoration.

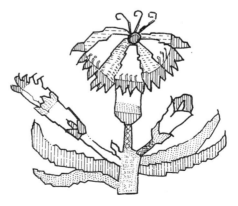

Tapestries were now widely produced in many European countries for palaces and great houses. James I founded the Mortlake factory near London in 1613 and encouraged the planting of mulberry trees to stimulate the silk industry. The factory had a short but definite influence on other English textiles, especially since both the designs and the workers were brought in from abroad. Charles I also patronised tapestry weaving and commissioned Rubens to design a series depicting the History of Achilles. In France, Louis XIV set out to create a unique palace at Versailles and encouraged artists in every field, including tapestry. His financial wizard Colbert founded factories at Gobelins in 1662, and Beauvais in 1664. In 1689 another factory was set up in London, this time in Soho. Large needlework hangings were often made, however, in imitation, or to rival weaving. A fine early series of Spanish tent stitch hangings of c.1600 in the Metropolitan Museum, New York depicts the History of Galcerán de Pinós. A later French example in the Musée Nissim de Camondo in Paris depicts a characteristic Louis XIV trophy—a huge group of weapons, armour and banners. Another of similar form at Versailles, after a design by Le Brun and worked in a convent, is even more elaborate. In Italy likewise, large pictorial hangings embroidered in silk were made, imitating tapestries. A fine set is to be seen at Hampton Court Palace and Windsor Castle. Other Italian needlework did not so much imitate as provide an alternative to tapestries. These sometimes showed religious events such as scenes from the lives of saints.

Louis XIV clearly liked needlework; he had a considerable amount made for Versailles, including furnishings for two of the most important rooms, the Throne Room and the King's Bedchamber. Most was ornamental rather than pictorial and consisted of formalised patterns ranging from complex arabesques to massive trophies. The Throne Room was hung with gold and silver hangings with architectural perspectives worked in high relief and 'after the fashion of marble'. The King's embroiderer Simon Delobel and others were employed for twelve years on furnishings for the King's Bedchamber. Sadly, nothing of this now survives; the needlework was exposed and prone to natural deterioration as well as to later raiding and destruction. The professionals involved in such works and in costume embroidery belonged to various guilds, but court workers were exempt from most regulations.

In England there was not as great a demand for grandiose palatial decoration; displays of riches were certainly made but in more domestic and less formal respects. Costume was flamboyant and lavish but there was a conscious attempt to prevent extravagance from becoming a general fashion, spreading through the classes. James I forbade a servant girl to wear: 'tiffany, velvet; lawns of white wires on the head, or about the kerchief, koyfe, crest cloth, but only linen; no farthingale, the ruff restricted to four yards in length before the gathering or setting of it'.

Plate 13a (top)
Russian coffin cover made in Moscow, 1678. Gold, pearls, jewels and bright silks are combined in superb craftsmanship to create an intense depiction of Christ's entombment and portraits of saints.

Plate 13b (bottom)
17th-century panel with a variety of spot motifs including birds, animals and fruit.

Figure 42
Large Italian silk needlework hanging, partly
enriched with silver
thread, depicting St
Anthony of Padua
preaching and St Francis
with the Trinity above.
*c.*1680. (17 ft x 11 ft).

By the middle of the century, noblemen's costumes were often more
elaborate and ornate in embroidery than their ladies'. Full length
portraits show them in complicated, sumptuous garments, trimmed
with rich lace ruffs and cuffs, and with rosettes on their shoes. With
military costume they wore needlework scarves, and a splendid surviving
example is one in the Victoria and Albert Museum said to have been

worn by Charles I at the battle of Edgehill. In contrast, Caroline ladies developed a taste for plain, though costly and beautiful, silks decorated only with lace. The superb colours and sheens of these have been captured in the portraits of the period.

This change in fashion caused needlework to become more specifically a pastime and hobby; girls devoted their energies towards making samplers, pictures and caskets for the dual purpose of general practice in sewing and for fun. Many new pattern books became available to inspire them, and artists were called upon to transcribe designs. In the accounts of Lady Shuttleworth of Gawthorpe (1619) it is recorded that the steward paid 2s. 4d. to Mr Bradell 'for drowing a waste coate and a night cappe'. Curiously, Mr Bradell was a distinguished and rich neighbour, and Receiver General to the King for the Duchy of Lancaster. He must have been accomplished in drawing as well, and been keen to help embroiderers. In general, most motifs were collated in pattern books, with wide circulation, and not much variation. Designs were adapted from these to linen, canvas, satin and other materials for working. Apart from the arrangement of them, there was little originality, but they nonetheless have great charm. A delightful set of panels at Traquair, Peeblesshire, shows a variety of fruit, flowers and creatures clearly derived from woodcuts and presumably intended for cutting out and applying to hangings.

Figure 43
Detail of a stumpwork picture showing motifs derived from pattern books. *c.*1670.
(18 in x 13½ in).

PATTERN BOOKS

Seventeenth-century pattern books essentially carried on the tradition established by those of the late 16th century, with sources such as Gerard de Jode's *Thesaurus Sacrarum Historiarum Veteris Testamenti* (Antwerp 1585). Their charming titles and illustrations conjure up a magical atmosphere that must have made fingers itchy for sewing: *A Book of Beast, Birds, Flowers, Fruits, Flies and Wormes, exactly drawne with their Lively Colours truly Described* by Thomas Johnson was published in 1630. It consisted of engravings borrowed from English, Dutch and German sources, printed in unrelated scales, the cause of similar discrepancies in needlework renderings. Richard Shorleyker's *A Schole House for the Needle* (1624) was very popular. The second edition indicates how adaptable the patterns were intended to be: 'sundry sorts of spots as Flowers, Birds, and Fishes, etc, and will fitly serve to be wrought, some with Gould, some with Silke, and some with Crewell, or otherwise at your pleasure'. James Boler's *The Needle's Excellency* (1631) was printed in many editions and was prefaced by 'the water poet', John Taylor's poem *The Prayse of the Needle*, which is full of information of contemporary needlework.[4] Another delightful title was *The History of four-footed beasts and serpents. Whereunto is now added the Theater of Insects* (1658). Peter Stent published a *Booke of Flowers Fruits Beastes Birds and Flies* in 1650. Twelve years later he was advertising, in addition, over 500

engraved prints in sheet form ranging from portraits of kings and queens to the seasons, senses and continents, as well as natural history subjects. Picture books of Bible stories and emblems were also available. Lions, leopards, elephants, unicorns, stags and camels often found their way into needlework, usually as curiosities, but occasionally with symbolic significance. The Cutlers' Company had twelve cushions 'with oliphants', clearly in this case an heraldic reference to their arms which displayed an Elephant and Castle crest and two elephants as supporters.

Some flowers and fruit were particularly favoured and often represented; some had emblematic overtones. Strawberries suggested purity and righteousness, pansies, meditation and carnations (or pinks), love. The last were derived from Persian ornament and appear even more frequently than roses, the old badge of state. In the insect world, moths hinted of the transitoriness of human life, snails of laziness, silk worms of industry, and bees of diligence and orderliness. Huish suggested that the caterpillar was a badge of Charles I.[5]

The oak and acorn were certainly associated with this king and also Charles II, who hid in an oak tree after the battle of Worcester; these are frequently seen, as are oak leaves and oak apples. Figs and pineapples, tulips and thistles are also found on 17th-century samplers. In the bird world, pelicans represented piety, pecking their breasts to release blood to succour their young. Ostriches were supposed to be able to eat iron; one is depicted in the Oxburgh hangings with a horseshoe in its mouth. The peacock was a symbol of Christ as eternal life and resurrection. It was thought that its flesh never decayed. Pairs of peacocks are often

shown flanking a fountain and standing in vines. A related device is seen in many samplers and the origin, though obscure, is probably ancient.

None of these motifs should however be too strongly emphasised as symbolic since it is likely that they were often chosen at random or by convention, irrespective of earlier meanings and nuances.

SAMPLERS

Though sampler-making had become a fully developed aspect of sewing, few survive from before 1650. There were earlier references in inventories and literature as mentioned in the previous chapter, but it was in the 17th century that samplers reached a peak of excellence before developing into decorative conventional forms in the 18th and 19th centuries. A good number have survived from the second half of the 17th century, regarded as heirlooms, and sentimental mementos of a previous generation. Many were signed and dated. Some were kept safely rolled up in work boxes, and others were protected by being framed and glazed.

They were sometimes worked by women but more often by teenagers, at home and in schools, as part of their basic education and as a training for marking linen and doing other domestic sewing. They were always

Figure 45
Two 17th-century botanical 'slips' for applying to bed curtains or other furnishings.

Figure 46
An unusual lace sampler partly worked with coloured and silver threads.

neat, of precise workmanship and showed experiments and records of colour combinations, in addition to patterns with exquisite detailing. Religious texts appear from the middle of the century, a moral aspect that shows a change in attitude to sampler-making from purely practical exercises to objects in themselves. Puritan ethics no doubt saw them as a prevention from idleness and thereby laid the foundations of the misery that was to be borne by some children in struggling with tedious set works with pious texts.

Seventeenth-century samplers (*Plates 15 & 16*) were usually worked on long narrow lengths of bleached, or unbleached, linen about 6–8 in (15–20 cm) wide and of various lengths, in rare cases even up to about 3 ft (1 m) or more. Length allowed for many strips or bands of border patterns; width was unnecessary as these were repetitive. They were embroidered with white and coloured silks and metal threads. Cut and drawn work was usually in white. Referred to in Taylor's poem as 'Italian Cutworke' and 'Frost-worke', it was increasingly popular, and culminated in contemporary needlepoint lace. It was particularly used on ruffs and cuffs as well as other items of costume, chiefly in geometric patterns. Whitework figures and animals are occasionally seen in samplers and sometimes pieces of needlepoint lace are incorporated. Samplers entirely of whitework are seldom dated.

The border patterns, texts and motifs were worked in parallel bands, as a result the term 'band sampler' is often used. The linen was imported and fairly expensive, so the bands were packed closely together; each was short, concise and compact. The patterns were of formal designs and contrasted. They were sometimes interspersed with other motifs, smaller floral and geometrical patterns. Flowers depicted included some of those already mentioned—roses, pansies, carnations, honeysuckle— with strawberries, acorns, etc. Pea flowers and an open pod motif are often seen. Any animals were of a stylised nature unless they were of the 'spot motif' type in which case they were realistically shaded.

Towards the end of the century, samplers taught not only sewing but alphabets, counting and religious texts. These features grew rapidly in popularity to become an essential part of sampler making. The earliest examples are not often signed, but some have initials, others a date; a few have both a signature and date. Occasionally, the age of the sewer is included and even worked into a little sentence. Huish cited an example: 'Mary Hall is my name and when I was thirteen years of age I ended this in 1662'. In the course of the next two centuries it became unusual not to have either a name or date. Sometimes these details on 17th-century ones are upside down in relation to the rest of the sampler. 'Boxers' were a curious feature and appeared usually in pairs. Possibly derived from a European motif of lovers exchanging gifts, they are small figures, either naked, or in shorts, or with contemporary costume, and apparently have wings, which prompts some to suggest that they are an adaptation of cherubs or putti, as in 16th-century Italian work.

Plate 15a (p. 70, left)
A mid-17th century spot motif sampler with a rich variety of patterns worked in brights silks and silver and gilt bullion.

Plate 15b (p. 70, right)
Another sampler with pictorial stag and lion motifs familiar in stump-work and derived from bestiaries or pattern books.

69

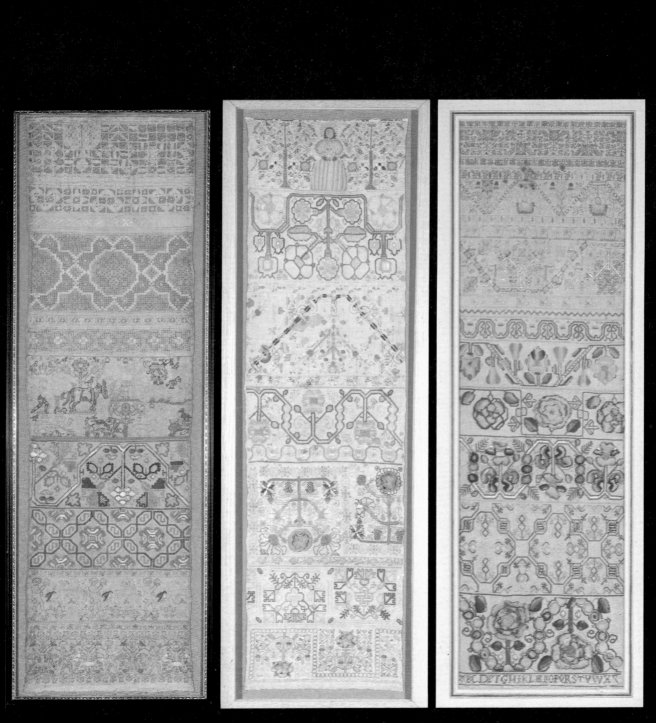

They always face out and have either straight hair or curly, like a wig. With one foot forward, they hold up in an enlarged hand an apparently strange object, (possibly flowers). They are invariably depicted between highly stylised tree motifs, thought to be a corruption of corresponding female figures.

Sometimes portions of overall pattern were included, in colourful flame stitch, or in scale or diaper patterns for example. Geometric patches of such are found on random or 'spot' motif samplers where a number of animal, flower or pattern motifs are spotted irregularly over a piece of linen. These motifs are at times included at one end of a band sampler, as for example one with animals and fish at the top, but more often spot motif samplers were limited to a combination of small pictures only. Animals, birds and insects already mentioned are typical of this genre, shown at random and unrelated in scale. Lions, kingfishers, caterpillars, human figures and plants were also depicted and all were in realistic, shaded colours, interspersed with beautifully stitched fragments of darning or border patterns. Heraldic devices, embossed metal thread work, and occasionally padded stumpwork are found too, and sometimes sequins, beads and pearls.

Crowns were another popular motif and the idea was probably introduced from Europe. Sometimes they are drawn and labelled in series of status with initials K (King), D (Duke), M (Marquis), E (Earl), V (Viscount), but often they were used simply to fill up lines of lettering or numerals.

A few interesting samplers recorded historic events. Huish describes three, commemorating William of Orange's arrival in England, his defeat of the French in 1692, and an earthquake in the same year. In this last one, Mary Minshall sewed: 'There was an earthquake on the 8 of September 1692 in the City of London but no hurt tho it caused most part of England to tremble'.

It is an indication of how American needlework in an English tradition was well established early in the 17th century that the first recorded American sampler was made in about 1635. By Loara Standish, it is in much the same form as English ones of the period, but interestingly has a verse recording her name and showing a dutiful approach to her task as one leading to virtue and religious piety.

There were many common features in the samplers of Great Britain and European countries. German, Dutch, Italian and French ones each have similarities. German samplers, often square in shape, were usually of fine cross-stitch and were neatly finished on both sides of the material. An early one, dated 1618, has columns of stitching in red and green silks, and other parts show cut and drawn work with needlepoint lace stitches.

Dutch samplers were originally about 25 in (64 cm) x 12 in (30 cm), or were long and thin, depending on loom sizes. Later they became a more standard 18 in (46 cm) square. They were often characterised by a border

Plate 16a (p. 71, left)
17th-century sampler with whitework at one end, animal motifs in outline form and 'boxers' in the lower bands.

Plate 16b (p. 71, centre)
A sampler with a portrait of a woman in the top band, c.1650.

Plate 16c (p. 71, right)
Another sampler, c.1650 with roses worked in relief and with an alphabet at the base.

surround, with spot motifs in the centre. Tulips, as an exotic novelty, were depicted together with flowers, windmills, animals, biblical motifs and a variety of lettering, though this was sometimes omitted.

The Italians were especially known for whitework, and their samplers in this form were worked with beautiful, elaborate designs which were considerably more complex and finer than similar techniques subsequently developed in other countries.

Early French samplers are not often found as they were probably less frequently made. They were usually signed at the bottom, but were otherwise similar to English ones.

Figure 47 a & b
A very rare pair of late 17th-century samplers by Alice and 'Margrett' Jennings, with similar motifs in white and polychrome work. Dated 1692 and 1695.

Figure 48
A fine 17th-century spot motif sampler worked in coloured silks and metal threads. *c.*1625.

EMBROIDERED PICTURES AND STUMPWORK

Girls made at least one sampler, often progressing to other works such as needlework pictures, small cabinets or caskets covered with needlework, and exercises in beadwork. A remarkable series of pieces worked by Martha Edlin has survived. Firstly, at the age of eight, she completed a coloured sampler in 1668. In the following year, she did one in whitework. In 1671, she finished a casket depicting the Seven Virtues, with Music and the Elements, and in 1673 a beadwork jewel box of which the lid only has survived.

Pictorial embroidery was popular in the Elizabethan period for cushions but by the middle of the 17th century much larger numbers of small panels were made in fine tent stitch and in raised padded work, which was given the name stumpwork in the 19th century. There was a small amount of raised work in Elizabethan embroidery, and more in Jacobean. But the fashion for padded embroidery was chiefly derived from the more serious sculptural use of the technique in European ecclesiastical vestments following the late middle ages. German baroque and Hungarian vestments were also highly embossed, like metalwork or carved wood; they were frequently encrusted with seed pearls, another feature adopted by English stumpwork, though in much smaller quantities.

These small pictures enjoyed a tremendous vogue. A large number of beautifully worked ones have been preserved, partly because they were framed and behind glass. They were always of amateur workmanship; the standardised subjects have a childish naivety and sameness that some generations have thought ludicrous, but others charming. The various kinds of picture show great patience and technical skill. The designs were similar, though tent stitch verions are apt to be more orderly with fairly coherent compositions and related vignettes. Stumpwork pictures display a collection of motifs, haphazardly associated, with little or no unity. Both were made up of conventional 'spots'.

Mirror frames and caskets (small cabinets with drawers and lids), as well as pictures, were made up with a collection of smaller panels of the same style. All were of three basic varieties: finely worked tent stitch, flat silk embroidery (laid and couched), and raised stumpwork. The last two were done on cream satin, though the flat silk stitching often covered the whole surface. In pictures, the satin background was sometimes dotted with sequins or tiny tendrils of embroidery. The same subjects were also sometimes worked in coloured glass beads; pictures, caskets, mirror frames, and other items in this form, give us an idea of the original colouring of their embroidered contemporaries, most of which have inevitably faded somewhat. The glass beads are of course of really vivid colours, interesting and lovely in their own way, but having a hardness which contrasts with the subtler shades that the embroideries have developed. Some caskets have been remarkably well

Figure 49
17th-century mirror with elaborate beadwork border.

preserved and many still have their original oak boxes in which they were protected. These were made by a professional cabinetmaker, or upholsterer, who was employed to make up the caskets from the needlework panels supplied by their maker. A charming note inside Hannah Smith's box (Whitworth Art Gallery, Manchester) written by her, records how her needlework was sent up to London from Oxford for this purpose: '. . . I was almost 12 years of age; when I went I made an end of my cabbinette, at Oxford . . . and my cabinet, was made up, in the year of 1656 at London'. This casket is also interesting for the representative variety of techniques employed in its workmanship. The doors are of fine tent stitch, and a stumpwork lion and leopard are on the canted angle parts around the top. The top itself is of flat silk stitches with metal thread; seed pearls are used for a necklace and crown. Another charming box, by Hannah Trapham, with her name and the date 1671 engraved on a silver catch, is at Sudbury Hall, Derbyshire. Later, caskets, mirror frames and pictures were often trimmed with tortoise-shell mouldings.

The main themes depicted in all these objects were largely derived from tapestries and, perhaps, bed valances, also, from Flemish and Dutch engravings. They were usually classical or religious but, despite this, a sense of humour is suggested in curious combinations of homely rabbits and insects cavorting alongside the solemn protagonists of Old Testament stories, or Ovid. An ambitious portrayal of Pharaoh's crossing of the Red Sea (at the Lady Lever Art Gallery, Port Sunlight) in the clumsy terms of stumpwork is full of amusing drama and chaos.

New Testament subjects were not yet fashionable; they were too 'religious' for Protestantism whereas the stories of the prophets were accepted as quaint and 'historical'. Bible stories represented particularly frequently include the following:

Adam and Eve	Genesis I
Abraham and the Angels	Genesis XVIII
Abraham and Hagar with Ishmael	Genesis XXI
The Sacrifice of Isaac	Genesis XXII
Rebekah	Genesis XXIV
Joseph and Potiphar	Genesis XXXIX
Moses in the Bulrushes	Exodus II
Jael and Sisera	Judges IV
David and Goliath	1 Samuel XVII
David and Abigail	1 Samuel XXV
David and Bathsheba	2 Samuel XI
The Judgement of Solomon	1 Kings III
Solomon and the Queen of Sheba	2 Chronicles IX
Jehu and Jezebel	2 Kings IX
Esther and King Ahaznerus	Esther II
Judith and Hofernes	Apocrypha
Susannah and the Elders	Apocrypha

Other works showed the seasons, the senses, the elements and portraits. Like 16th-century valances, these were all depicted in 'modern dress' and the chief prophets, kings and queens were always in the form of Charles I and Henrietta Maria. Charles I had become a cult figure, king and martyr, and it is interesting to notice that though he and his Queen were repeatedly shown in allegorical terms, Charles II and James II were not.

Extraordinary trouble was taken in perfecting minutely worked pictures. In the Victoria and Albert Museum a version of King Solomon receiving the Queen of Sheba shows the use of real hair and crowns of gold set with pearls. The silk and gold thread canopy has loosely hanging movable curtains of embroidered old brocade; the figures are adorned with strings of real pearls and lace. Three dimensional effects were achieved by stuffing individual embroidered pieces with wool, hair, cloth or pieces of wood, while hands and faces were of wax, wood, bone (or ivory), painted satin and, in the finest examples, of split stitch with the tiny features in stem stitch. Windows in buildings and the water in ponds and fountains were represented by pieces of mica (talc). Some caskets contain, or have on the top, a garden of free-standing flowers and ornaments; one of this type has a garden or meadow with figures, a shepherdess under a tree, sheep, other trees and a wild rose. Many have flapping leaves with shadows behind them worked in flat stitching. Later, Charles II stumpwork was less padded, giving way increasingly to flat and laid stitch work.

Figure 52
Stumpwork picture
depicting a king receiving
a queen, with attendants
and many other typical
motifs. *c.*1670.

The variety of method was almost infinite, though the range of subjects was limited. The curiously disassociated juxtaposition of 'curiosities', mythological, religious, natural historical and even heraldic, in unrelated scales, combined in creating an atmosphere of magic or fantasy.

Tent-stitch pictures were rather more orderly, as I have intimated. The designs must have been drawn out by professionals; some were printed and some were directly derived from engravings.[6] A small, finely worked panel at Alnwick Castle, Northumberland, depicting galleons engaged in battle at sea, with Neptune and nymphs in the foreground, must have been copied or adapted from an old print, the subject already being considered quaint and historic. Some pictures of the 1660s onwards were embroidered in wool only, in long flat stitches, colourful and charming but of distinctly less intricate workmanship. A fine example in the Metropolitan Museum depicts familiar motifs including a king and a huge butterfly against a vivid background of red, green and blue. Two further examples, dated 1681, are at Glamis Castle.

An unusual picture at the Lady Lever Art Gallery commemorates the defeat of the Spanish Armada and the Gunpowder plot, with an inscription: 'To God in memory of his double deliverance from the invincible navie and the unmatchable powder treason'. This was a rendering by Dame Dorothy Selby from a popular print published in Amsterdam in

Plate 17
Mid-17th-century silk
tent-stitch picture of
King Solomon and the
Queen of Sheba with
attendant figures, all
represented in contem-
porary costume. Many
other frequently repeated
motifs are also included.

1621. Half worked examples are beautiful in themselves. One, depicting the story of Diana and Actaeon, shows precise drawing with no errors that could lead to confusion for the sewer, with motifs carefully and evenly spaced out. It would seem likely that the needleworker herself chose the subjects and incidental vignettes that the draughtsman incorporated. Had this not been the case, artists would have developed more obvious, perhaps duller, compositions.

Graceful needlework portraits of ladies were popular, often in an oval format surrounded by bands of metal purl (coiled silver wire), with additional features shown in the background and in spandrels. Small portraits were sometimes placed within a larger picture, or in the border of a mirror frame, with the lady perhaps holding a lute.

Miniature oval portraits of Charles I were made after engravings by Sir Anthony van Dyck (1599-1641). Some may have been made by professionals but many are said to be partly worked with the King's own hair, thereby to be regarded as true relics of Charles the Martyr. A version in the Victoria and Albert Museum has hair worked in with silks. The King was also frequently depicted in tent stitch pictures, (*Plate 20a*) almost always seated as in his official portraits, thereby concealing his short stature. A splendid bust portrait of Charles II in the Metropolitan Museum, boldly labelled as in a print 'Carolus II', depicts his lusty features and a magnificent dark wig.

Court art and decoration in Britain was considerably influenced by European workshops, though neither techniques nor styles deflected

Figure 53
A picture with spot motifs applied to cream satin, in original carved and silvered frame, *c.*1670.

Figure 54

Two central European
stumpwork pictures
depicting events in the
New Testament story of
the birth of Christ.

English girls from their passion for domestic pictures. In Holland landscapes, seascapes and still life flower groups were worked with the
needle in reflection of Dutch painting. A 'Landskipp peace done in
Holland—with a needle in Silke' was presented to Charles I, together
with other pictures, in 1635.

Edmund Harrison (1589–1666) who was embroiderer to James I,
Charles I and Charles II worked in a manner more typical of Flanders
than England. He may well have been trained there as he used especially
the technique of *or nué*, or shaded gold. He undertook and supervised
various work for court functions including masques, plays and heraldic
banners. We now have only some of his religious pictures, worked in
silk on canvas, in the form of needlepainting. His figures were done
separately, then applied to another fabric, as stumpwork, but they were
not padded. They have a sculptural quality as a result of the combination
of 'old master' subjects with the metallic nature of the *or nué* technique.
The Visitation, *The Betrothal* and *The Adoration*[7] were made for William
Howard, Lord Stafford; all are dated 1637.

Seventeenth-century embroidered bookbindings were usually decorated in the manner and form of pictures and were made by both
professionals and amateurs. Professionally made ones were usually for
presentation. At Windsor Castle there is a *Book of Common Prayer* of 1638
bound in blue velvet and embroidered on it the Prince of Wales' badge
of three feathers enclosed by the Garter, surmounted by a crown, with
the monogram C P worked in gold and silver thread. Charles II had
an embroiderer, John Morris, who undertook bindings, probably of a
formal nature.

Bookbindings generally fall into four categories. Firstly, there were
those of tent stitch, depicting religious and allegorical subjects, sometimes with a silver background. Secondly, there were ones with raised

work in a mixture of silks and metal threads on a velvet ground. Thirdly, there was silk embroidery on white satin, either in floral patterns or with oval portraits within flower borders, perhaps with metal threads, sequins and pearls. The spines of these would be decorated with flowers, animals or insects within sectional compartments. The fourth kind were those which were probably professionally made, decorated with heraldry, monograms and other formal patterns. Francis Bacon gave a copy of his *Essays* to the Duke of Buckingham with an embroidered portrait of the recipient in the centre of the dark green velvet cover (Bodleian Library).[8] Some bindings were partly inspired by the tooling of leather, with strapwork, cherub's heads, initials and a variety of spandrels.

Books were held closed either with silk ties or silver clasps. Many had bags to protect them which were large enough to hold them loosely; these were also finely worked, but not in relief, and with the same design on both sides. Silk and metal thread book markers, with coloured ribbons, plaited cords or tassels, were also made.

Small, tightly stuffed pillows or cushions were frequently made to hold prayerbooks and Bibles, or for other uses. They too were similarly decorated with pictorial or patterned motifs on one side only, sometimes with tassels and a fringe of gold or silver lace. (*Plate 14b*)

ORIENTAL INFLUENCES AND CREWELWORK

Large-scale wool embroideries, like the Bayeux Tapestry, had not been worked for over 500 years when there was at last a new development of the technique in the early 17th century. It appeared to happen inevitably that the coiling, monochrome flower patterns of Elizabethan costumes were enlarged and applied to great expanses for bed hangings. A skirt in the London Museum of a large blackwork pattern is almost identical in design to curtains, especially a set on a bed at Cothele House, Cornwall. In both cases the embroidery is of wool on linen twill, with circular tendrils containing real flowers. The wool was known as crewel ('crule', 'crewle' or 'croyl'), an inexpensive worsted yarn, closely twisted, of long staple wool with the fibres lying parallel. Its use was very ancient. The word crewel was originally pronounced as a monosyllable but in two syllables by the mid-16th century when it was also known as 'caddis', 'caddas', 'caddiz', 'caddice', etc. The linen twill was often homespun, with linen warps on cotton wefts, strong and less costly than imported materials.

Though much crewelwork of the 17th and 18th centuries must have been made in workshops, an equally large quantity was entirely made by amateurs. The cloth, spinning and dyeing could all be home produced and, indeed, the fashion for doing crewel embroidery soon became an absorbing passion amongst women, just as stumpwork was with their children. Pepys, the diarist, tells us that every woman, including his

Plate 18a (top)
Charles II stumpwork casket with raised and flat figures, flowers, animals, birds and insects, the interior is also embroidered and fitted with small drawers and a mirror, *c.*1660.

Plate 18b (bottom)
A beadwork picture, *c.*1670, showing a lady on hillocky ground and numerous slips, insects, birds and animals, and the initials 'E.L.'

wife, was involved in extensive projects on new 'furniture' for beds. It was laborious work but they covered ground relatively fast and had no background to fill in with the tedious tent stitch of canvas work. The finished effect was bold, colourful and baroque.

The patterns, as stated, originated from Elizabethan blackwork (monochrome, but not always black) but they were also considerably influenced by Flemish verdure tapestries with stylised curling leaves, and Venetian needlepoint lace which had similar leaves with characteristic infilling patterns that could be adapted to wool stitches. These had already influenced blackwork. There were also nuances of the leaf designs of French and Italian baroque silks which were bold, formalised and no longer naturalistic. But the greatest source of new ideas came from the Far East and these became especially apparent in the latter part of the century. Oriental exchanges of taste and technique gave our entire culture inestimable new stimulus in quality, design, colour and charm.

Venice and Portugal had carried on trade with the East since the Renaissance and England savoured a few magical imports. In 1600 the East India Company was incorporated by Elizabeth I's charter and this was endorsed by James I. Trading at Surat was agreed to by the consent of the Mughal rulers of the State of Gurjarat on the Coromandel coast of India in 1612 and a lively business exchange flourished for seventy-five years. In 1687 the Company transferred its headquarters to Bombay which had been ceded to England by Portugal as part of the dowry of Catherine da Braganza on her marriage to Charles II. Even the Lord Chancellor, Thomas Cromwell, little knew what far reaching results the deal would have, and when asked where the new territory was, merely replied: 'It is a paltry island a little distance off the coast of Brazil.' Extraordinary vagueness and an air of glamorous mystery surrounded the fabulous riches of the Orient. The 'Indian' provinces from which the superb luxuries of silks, embroideries, pearls, jewels, spices, perfumes, porcelain and lacquer were brought were regarded with the greatest fascination. These goods came from China and India, and many other places linked to the merchant routes. But all these countries were thought of as a single land bordered on the far side by a range of mountains which the flood had not covered. Beyond this was Cathay, a Paradise land. The precious merchandise was therefore valued as the magical elixir of a land bordering heaven, redolent with the romance of the beautiful and remote Garden of Eden.

Textiles imported from the Orient were very popular and gave new inspiration to English manufacturers. The earlier crewelwork curtains embroidered in the tradition of blackwork, had a single overall pattern, usually of leaves, endlessly repeated over the fabric with just a narrow border of the same pattern in a smaller form around the edges. The colours were originally monochrome, most often a deep blue-green, but subsequently of two shades such as blue-green with brown, combina-

Figure 55
Crewelwork curtain
worked in several shades
of blue-green on cotton-
linen twill. *c.*1670.

tions of blues and greens, red and black, and flame colours as seen on a
bed at Doddington Hall, Lincolnshire.[9] (See also *Plate 20*.) At the same
time a greater variety of stitches was used. It is in the next stage that
signs of direct Asian influence are noted, namely the conception of an
individual design for each curtain instead of a repeated pattern. This was
invariably based on the ancient tree of life motif, in the form of a semi-
natural, semi-stylised tree winding from the base all over the hanging to
its extremities. The idea was adopted from the first imports of Indian
pintadoes and palampores. At first they were of white designs on a
coloured ground, usually a deep red and painted or printed by a wax
process, but as these were not particularly well received in England, the
East India Company requested a reversal of the colour scheme, and
suggested the introduction of other colours. They even went so far as
to send out models 'in the Chinese taste' for copying in paint, print and
needlework. The mutually developed products enjoyed a colossal
success and European demand clearly helped shape the delightful
oriental 'export' items. In 1683 the directors of the East India Company
wrote to their suppliers in Surat saying that imported chintzes were
exceedingly popular and ordered a hundred sets of painted curtains for
immediate delivery. They reported that all but the very poorest in
England now had curtains and valances for their beds. They also
ordered large numbers of cushions: 'each bed to have 12 cushions for
chairs of the same work'. At first there was a market in India for English
needlework but the orientals quickly learned to imitate it, and made
their own competitive varieties.

Crewelwork patterns developed into exotic trees with luscious tropical
leaves, heavily curling on upward-winding branches from a rooted

base and growing out of undulating or hillocky ground. This last feature of Indian hangings may have originated from the stylised mountains and wave-like patterns around the base of Chinese robes; it certainly developed into the hillocky groundwork in later English tent stitch pictures. Much of the woolwork was dense and heavy in appearance but lighter designs were also carried out. A magnificent bed at Houghton Hall, Norfolk is hung with minutely worked polychrome embroidery, chiefly in chain-stitch. This and another similar set of hangings (*Plate 4*) show a wide variety of European and oriental flowering shrubs with magnificent birds, closely related to Chinese coromandel lacquer, wallpaper and Indian textiles.

Transposed Chinese and Indian influences such as these should be distinguished from a more playful and decorative aping of Chinese styles, known as chinoiserie. It was in a different spirit that Europeans began imitating oriental art, as closely as possible, but naturally somewhat superficially. It became the height of fashion and entertainment to embroider, paint and even do lacquerwork 'in the Indian manner' or 'in the Chinese taste', these terms being synonymous. English imitations of lacquer were known as Japaning and instructions for amateurs were laid out in Stalker and Parker's *Treatise of Japaning and Varnishing* (1688), which included a number of 'quaint' motifs. The desire for chinoiserie gathered momentum in furniture, tapestries, porcelain and crewelwork and by the 18th century it had become widely popular. An English silk bedcover, in the Victoria and Albert Museum, one of two similar ones, has chinoiserie motifs on it including rocks, trees, pavilions, pagodas and bridges. It is signed 'Sarah Thurstone' with the date 1694.

It is hard to assess which crewelwork was domestic and which professional but some examples are clearly homely. Abigail Pett's hangings in the Victoria and Albert Museum are signed by her. They consist of plant and animal motifs, drawn and spaced out over the fabric like stumpwork, but the plants are unreal, tropical and exotic, each growing from a characteristic Chinese rock formation. These craggy rocks, full of holes, like caves, are a principal feature of Chinese lacquer and textiles, and were adopted in Indian palampores. They became an important motif in chinoiserie being imitated in Italian and English garden grottos. John Nieuhof in *The Embassy to the Grand Tartar*, translated from Dutch in 1669, illustrates 'cliffs made by art'. A polychrome crewelwork fragment in Boston Museum of Fine Arts (USA) and the Ashburnham Indian hanging in the Victoria and Albert Museum are very closely related in design. Both have the craggy rock formation, similar stylised animals, oriental figures and European flowers. They show clearly the interrelationship of style in the two countries and their common derivation from Chinese sources.

Abigail Pett's needlework also shows birds and animals, a curious mixture of stumpwork lions and stags, with Chinese cranes and phoenixes. It was part of the rich decorative quality of crewelwork that it

Figure 56
One of a set of French crewelwork curtains with grotesques in the style of Jean Bérain. Late 17th or early 18th century.
(8 ft 5 in x 4 ft 2 in).

86

adapted and combined happily such diverse emblems. On occasions when flowers were less stylised, one can see a mixture of European and oriental varieties, including some of the Taoist and Buddhist symbols associated with the seasons. Spring is represented by magnolias and peonies, Summer by lotus flowers, Autumn by chrysanthemums and Winter by roses and prunus blossoms.

An ebony bed, associated with Catherine of Braganza, at Boughton House, Northamptonshire, is hung with interesting crewelwork of a vine pattern. The profuse bunches of grapes are worked in a kind of stumpwork.

The passion for crewelwork reached even the remotest parts of the country, as testified by a list made in the Orkneys in 1650 after the death of Lady Morton. This includes many fascinating items and reads like poetry, with delightful descriptions of fine quality pieces, and gives an indication of how much they were treasured. Items such as '1 Gryt Sweet Bagg soad with pitty point' and '2 Dosson fox skinns' are recorded but of crewelwork there was: '1 Whyt fustan bedd, sow'd with Incarnat worsett whereoff 15 pieces was of it'. That the needlework was red (incarnat) at this early date is interesting as the majority was of blue-greens. The fifteen pieces would have been made up of four or more curtains, three valances for the canopy, and three for the base, a head curtain, a lining for the canopy and a coverlet, with perhaps additional cushions.

The use of crewelwork was as an alternative to silks and velvets which were used on important beds over carved and padded mouldings in the manner of designs by Daniel Marot. This furniture was suitable for more formal surroundings and was especially made for royal palaces and other great houses. Several chairs of state, canopies and beds of this nature are still to be seen at Hampton Court Palace, Chatsworth and Knole. Silk needlework hangings are well represented by the splendid bed with a wing chair, side chairs and stools *en suite* at Clandon Park, Surrey. Made in about 1700 the brilliantly coloured silks depict a regular pattern of red and blue flowers on a cream background. The cost of such needlework was tremendous. About this time Lapierre, a leading upholsterer, charged the Duke of Devonshire £15 for a large bedstead and as much as £470 for the hangings.[10]

Another very fine bed, in this case of colossal height, is at Drayton House, Northamptonshire. It has tall 'paned' curtains and long narrow ones, *cantonières*, at the corners where the main curtains meet. The needlework of these and similar work on a set of six chairs (loose fitting covers) and a sofa is of a formal floral design, probably derived from Dutch engravings, in wool with silk highlights. Original bills suggest it was the work of Hugenot needlewomen around 1701.[11]

Florentine stitch hangings (*Plate 11b*) offered a stiffer form of decoration than most crewel designs. The bright wavy patterns, also known as Hungarian or flame stitch (the equivalent of the modern bargello),

Figure 57
The state bed, a fine wing chair, a side chair and stool, all with magnificent late 17th-century silk needlework. The carpet is of 18th-century needlework. (Clandon Park, Surrey).

have a timeless quality that has always been popular. The zig-zag stripes, or lozenges, were at first of untwisted silks, and later of wools, or of a mixture. They are reminiscent of marblised paper. A room at Chastleton House, Gloucestershire is hung with Florentine work and other magnificent examples at Parham Park are on a bed and as hangings. The same pattern was also achieved in a woven form.

Though on the whole uniquely English, crewelwork was also done in America, based on examples taken out to the New World from this country. Good embroidery of this kind was mostly produced in the 18th century but there are some earlier examples. A set of bed hangings of the late 17th century in the Metropolitan Museum is said to have been worked by the three successive wives of Dr Gilson Clapp. Embroidered in red wool, they show birds, squirrels, stags pierced with arrows, and floral sprays.

American 'Turkey work', needlework imitations of oriental carpets (not woven or hand knotted) were recorded as early as 1670 and were especially used for covering chairs, for table carpets and for bed covers.

Quilting had been used for a number of practical reasons and as decoration since the Middle Ages. The stitching bound together several layers to form pocketed insulation. Bed covers in this fashion[12] were made in mediaeval days and continued to be popular throughout the 17th century, though often 'false quilting' was done without any padding. The stitching was in complex geometric, vermicular and foliate patterns. Clothes were also quilted, especially jackets.

88

Quilting was especially developed in England, but almost certainly had an oriental origin and it is interesting that while many oriental needlework imports were looked upon suspiciously by apprehensive English workshops, Charles I pointedly permitted the importation of 'quilts of China'. In the 1614 inventory of Henry Howard, Earl of Northampton, several 'China quiltes' are listed, including one of a chequer pattern in yellow silk. Yellow, the Chinese imperial colour, was particularly popular and much used in Chinese, Portuguese and subsequent English quilting; frequently this work formed a background for coloured floral embroidery, usually in chain-stitch.

William and Mary gave their names to the decorative styles prevalent during the last part of the century. It was a period of great building programmes in England, epitomised by Wren, with high quality building, woodwork in large panelled rooms, Dutch and oriental style furniture and porcelain, rich upholstery and luxurious textiles. The court was splendid with uniforms. Even the rat-catcher had a professionally made costume: 'of crimson cloth lyned with blew serge and guarded with blew velvett Embroidered with their Maties W R M R and Crownes on back and chest and six Rattes Eateing a Wheat-sheave on the left shoulder'.

Figure 58
Charles I taking leave of his children, 29th January 1648. Probably derived from an engraving and signed 'Mary Middleton Ended this work October th 31. 1741'. (22½ in x 22 in).

Queen Mary herself was known for her needlework and was to be seen doing it everywhere, even in her carriage as it passed. Celia Fiennes in the 18th century visited Windsor Castle and noted: 'hangings, chaires, stooles and screen the same, all of satten stitch done in worsteads, beasts, birds, ymages and ffruites all wrought very ffinely by Queen Mary and her Maids of Honour'. There was another set by her at Hampton Court Palace which may have been of knotting as she loved this technique also. Linen threads were knotted with a shuttle and then couched down in complicated patterns, especially suitable for formal furnishings. Red strapwork designs in knotting were applied to yellow silk upholstery on a large number of chairs and stools at Ham House. Some unused pieces show how brilliant the original unfaded effect was. Knotting was also done in metal threads for formal patterns on important canopies, hangings and upholstery. Also, at Ham House, there is an example of couched cord and applied work in the Blue Drawing Room, on a set of wall hangings of damask, paned with dark blue velvet.

By the end of the 17th century canvas work re-emerged as a form for hangings in anticipation of the many uses of this type of needlework on 18th-century furniture. A series of large panels found in a house in Hatton Garden (now in the Victoria and Albert Museum) show a curious mixture of crewelwork-type leaves around columns with the familiar animals below, including lions and unicorns.

NOTES

Epigram: Chaucer, *The Book of the Duchess*, 252–3.

1 A similar panel in the Cooper-Hewitt Museum, New York is thought to be Italian or Spanish.

2 Therle Hughes, *English Domestic Needlework*, n.d., p. 21.

3 Included in Frank Partridge exhibition catalogue, 1934.

4 Quoted on the end papers of *The Needleworker's Dictionary*, Pamela Clabburn 1976.

5 Marcus B. Huish, *Samplers and Tapestry Embroideries*, 1900.

6 *Apollo* February, 1977. Margaret H. Swain, 'Embroidered Pictures from Engraved Sources', citing examples in the Burrell Collection.

7 Fitzwilliam Museum, Cambridge, Royal Scottish Museum, Edinburgh, Victoria and Albert Museum, London respectively.

8 Bacon's awareness of needlework is reflected in his Essay no. V *Of Adversity*: '... Prosperity is not without many fears and distastes; and adversity is not without comforts and hopes. We see in needleworks and embroideries, it is more pleasing to have a lively work upon a sad and solemn ground, than to have a dark and melancholy work upon a lightsome ground: judge, therefore of the pleasure of the heart by the pleasure of the eye.'

9 A modern bed hung with early coral-red crewelwork is at Stonor Park, Oxfordshire.

10 The inside of the canopy of a great blue bed at Burghley House, Northamptonshire, is decorated with strapwork mouldings decorated with embroidery.

11 See guidebook to Drayton House by Gervase Jackson-Stops.

12 Quilts are listed in spellings varied from *cowltes* to *qwhiltez*. The word is derived from the Latin *culcita*, a stuffed sack, mattress or cushion.

5 The Eighteenth Century

The pattern grows, the well depict'd flower
Unfolds its bosom, buds and leaves and sprigs,
And curling tendrils, gracefully disposed,
Follow the nimble fingers of the fair.

HE QUEEN ANNE and Georgian periods are celebrated for exceptional elegance and quality in almost every field. Architecture, and especially the decorative arts, produced a quantity of perfectly proportioned works, in both standard and unusual forms, in a progression of contrasting styles. Strangely perfect coincidences of stimulus and influence, the man and the moment, made the 18th century England's greatest period of decorative creativity. Though the origins of the baroque, rococo, chinoiserie and neo-classical tastes came from outside the country, the styles evolved here were, in essence, distinctly English. This was especially the case with needlework which attained a secular domestic peak, derived from many sources, while retaining its characteristically idiosyncratic nature.

At the outset of the century, Parliament attempted to curb the importation of all materials 'of China, Persia, or the East Indies' as these threatened the prosperity of the English silk industry. In 1720 foreign coloured embroidery was prohibited, and even cotton goods were specified in the following year. These restrictions were relaxed in 1736, but in 1749 metal thread embroidery, lace and fringes were forbidden on the grounds of national economy. Venice had inspired a considerable use of metal threads, and 'purl' was much used. This appears in records from early in the 16th century and throughout the 17th and 18th, with a variety of meanings from metal bobbles looking like stringed pearls, to gold thread lace. Basically, it was finely coiled gold wire, flexible enough to be couched down in various patterns. The heaviest purl was referred to as bullion. A cheaper form, of copper, was known as silk purl. This did not merit 'drizzling' or 'parfilage', the practice of raiding supposedly old or unwanted garments for reusable materials. Metal threads continued to be fashionable on costume throughout the 18th century, often stiffening and weighting down the garment. Jewels were not used, partly as silk and metal threads were now so lustrous, and partly as there was a tendency for elegance instead of the former studied grandeur. There were exceptions, appropriately, of oriental splendour. We are told, for instance, that Louis XV, at the age of eleven, received the Sultan of Turkey's ambassador 'in a suit of flame coloured velvet, weighed down with nearly 40 pounds in weight of jewels'. The swankery of Elizabethan status symbols was continuously practised in eastern countries. French embroidery, however, though consistently more formal in style than English, was increasingly done by amateur ladies. Madame de Maintenon, wife of Louis XIV, founded an embroidery school at the Convent of St Cyr where she retired after the King's death. Daughters of the aristocracy were sent here to learn needlework, especially the canvas embroidery known today as *point de St Cyr*.

Italian vestments, in the meanwhile, followed the fashion of baroque architecture in which flamboyance was the touchstone of a worldly, almost hedonistic, conception for glorious churches. Workshops in Rome were celebrated for needlework almost exclusively of gold, the patterns being of a bold scrolling form, sometimes with additional bright colours. An Italian altar frontal at Anglesey Abbey is decorated almost entirely with secular motifs—fat spiralling columns richly decorated with flowers, vast urns of flowers, winged cupids holding baskets with more, and a large variety of birds in the air and on the ground.

Religious subjects were frequently more prominent in domestic 18th-century needlework than in important ecclesiastical pieces. Carriage seat cushions in southern Sweden were embroidered with Adam and Eve or other religious motifs, and in most countries, throughout the century, Bible stories were portrayed in homely needlework pictures.

After the 17th century, the development of needlework turned from an emphasis on children's work, pictures and caskets, to a preponderance of canvas work. More needlework was done for practical purposes such as covering furniture. It was increasingly adult in approach and designs were based on a very wide range of subjects, classical and Bible stories, mythology, fables, chinoiserie and others. Towards the end of the 18th century, canvas work was less popular, being replaced by silk embroidery of a purely decorative nature. The bolder tent and cross stitch floral patterns gave way to light silken ones. These, in turn, were followed by plainer geometric designs in canvaswork, the simpler lines being more attuned to neo-classicism and Sheraton-style furniture.

Throughout the century needlework was held in high esteem as a serious amateur pursuit. Most women did needlework and enjoyed it, and many men as well. Louis XV himself was proud of his abilities in this field. An amusing correspondence in *The Spectator* in 1714 sheds light on the strong views held by the older generation about doing needlework. A woman wrote to that paper on October 13th complaining of her young nieces' lack of desire to do useful and productive embroidery as their forbears had done. She encouraged the paper to take a lead in encouraging its readers in this direction: 'For my part, I have plied my needle these fifty years, and would never have it out of my hand. It grieves my heart to see a couple of proud, idle flirts sipping their tea, for a whole afternoon, in a room hung with the industry of their great-

Figure 59
Christ and the woman of Samaria, probably derived from a bible illustration, *c.*1730. (18½ in x 17½ in).

grandmother. . .' The editor somewhat mockingly replied that he was
sure that all ladies would shortly 'appear covered in the work of their
owns hands . . . How pleasing is the amusement of walking the shades
and groves planted by themselves, in surveying heroes slain by their
needle. . .' He obviously felt that the advocated designs—those dense
entanglements of herbage—were inappropriate.

Pictorial subjects were increasingly popular from the latter part of
the 17th century, and in the 18th century they show further naturalism.
This then led to a decorative, ornamental approach. Garden ornaments
such as urns, obelisks, fountains, statues and baskets of flowers were
repeated hallmarks. Arrangements of flowers packed closely together,
derived probably from Dutch paintings, were often charmingly shown
in Chinese or Delft blue and white vases.[1] (*Plate 1*) Unlike the Elizabethan
and Stuart fashion for showing plants growing from the ground, 18th-
century needlework usually shows cut flowers in arrangements or in
posies.

Wool had been much used in crewelwork hangings and Queen Anne
pictures were often worked in worsteds, rather than silks, but silks were
used for highlighting. The designs, though more realistic, still combined curiously impossible collections of subjects. English landscape
hillocks are host to lions, leopards, camels, parrots and oriental pheasants. With these are depicted figures in Eastern or European costume
and homely oak trees, sheep and squirrels. A splendidly documented
panel at Mellerstain, Berwickshire is signed with the initials of two
Menzies sisters and their governess and dated 1706. A portrait of a
lady with flowers, representing the sense of smell, is taken from an
engraving. This is surrounded by flower and fruit slip motifs with birds,
animals and insects derived from *A Booke of Beast, Birds, Flowers, Fruits,
Flies and Wormes* . . . published by Thomas Johnson in 1630. The engraving of *Smelling* and this book, bound together, are still near the
needlework panel in Lord Haddington's collection at Mellerstain.[2]

Needlework portraits of monarchs continued to be made, closely
following engravings of official portraits. Charles I was still a cult figure;
two very similar pictures, after Bower's painting of the king at his trial,
are signed and dated with enigmatic variation. (*See Plate 20a* for one;
the other, belonging to Sir John Carew Pole, Bart, Antony House,
Cornwall, is signed 'Anna Skinner in the 68th year of her age, 1715'). A
large silk picture of Queen Anne in the Metropolitan Museum, New York,
depicts her as she was always represented, wearing her coronation robes.
Similar formal portraits were made of the three Georges and their queens.

Though such pictures retained many features typical of the 17th
century, designs grew more florid as the 18th century progressed.
Costume, furniture, fabrics and panels became brighter and more
elegant. The feeling of tidy woodcuts disappeared and luxuriant garden
flowers spread with profusion in needlework for a period of about fifty
years. Around 1770 these were superseded by another reflection of

Figure 61
An 18th-century panel,
the background of floss
silks, the flowers, birds
and animals in tent and
rococo stitches. (Detail.)
(23 in x 17½ in).

engraving, this time having a delicate, copper plate flimsiness. In general, however, a love of natural things led to a passion for 'arcadia'. Elegant rural interpretations were given to old illustrations and, unlike in the previous century, efforts were made to depict figures in the realistic dress of their period. Pastoral subjects were especially popular though others were still drawn from Cleyn's illustrations for Virgil's *Aeneid* and *Eclogues and Georgics* (Ogilvy's translations of 1658 and 1654). Arcadian scenes, in needlework, were spread throughout the house, interpersed with billowing floral patterns, curling leaves and tendrils. Celia Fiennes described a house in Epsom:

> You enter one roome hung with crosstitch in silks . . . window curtaines white satin silk damaske with furbellows of callicoe printed flowers, the chairs crosstitch, the two stooles of yellow mohaire with crosstitch true lovers Knotts in straps along and across, an elbow chaire tentstitch . . . many fine pictures under glasses of tentstitch, satinstitch gumm and straw work also Indian flowers and birds.

These latter Indian motifs refer us back to crewelwork.

By the second quarter of the 18th century crewelwork designs were less crowded, more elegant and colourful, though they lost something of their former boldness. Tree tendrils became thinner, more evenly spaced and regularly meandering. They also now had flowers of English or Indian origin with the formalised leaves which were less fat, though long and languidly curling. The range of stitches was limited and simplified, chain-stitch alone sometimes replaced the former complex variety. In addition to tree patterns, bed curtains were also decorated with smaller groups of flowers, formalised asparagus leaves and other motifs. Crewelwork designs and techniques were used for dresses and bags as well as for beds. Occasionally the same design is found worked on both crewel curtains and in tent stitch embroidery, such as seat coverings. A set of hangings at Knebworth House, Hertfordshire, is worked in beads in a design typical of crewelwork.

American needlework was at its best in the 18th century and included fine crewelwork. On the whole, embroidery in the USA was a luxury for those who could afford the time and the materials; most time had to be devoted to productive work such as farming the land, while tools and cloth were still relatively scarce. Items made were chiefly of a practical nature with clear household uses. They included rugs, bell-pulls, chair seats and bed hangings but costumes were also sewn with crewelwork designs of a pastoral nature as inappropriate as the ones *The Spectator* had ridiculed. In 1749 a stolen garment was reported as '... a Woman's Fustian Petticoat, with large work'd Embroider'd Border, being Deer, Sheep, Houses, Forrests, etc ...' A large reward was offered for its recovery. American crewelwork designs were usually similar to the English ones from which they were derived but were considerably lighter in feeling; bed hangings especially were less densely embroidered, partly on account of a shortage of wools. Local plants and animals were incorporated sometimes. Indigo was a home product of the American colonies and was much used in shades of dark to light blue, blended with other colours, or by themselves, especially in New England.

Figure 62
American long panel with a typically naive design and characteristic workmanship. New England, *c.* 1750.

By 1750 rich velvets, silks, damasks and brocades were so much the taste, in conjunction with elaborately carved and gilded furniture, that needlework hangings seemed less attractive. Crewelwork fell out of favour and the energies of embroideresses were turned to tent stitch carpets, wall hangings and furniture coverings, or to making pictures. Bed hangings of silk were occasionally made, of extreme fineness and at great cost. Two sets were made by professional embroideresses for Queen Charlotte. The first was for Windsor Castle and showed accurately depicted flowers on satin. It took Mrs Wright fourteen years to complete. The second was for Hampton Court Palace, where it can still be seen. Of lilac silk it was again profusely and minutely embroidered with realistic flowers in brilliant silks, and was made in 1775-8 by Mrs Pewsey, also known for starting a school of needlework at Aylesbury.

A number of magnificent coverlets of the Queen Anne and George I periods were probably also professionally made. Sometimes with sets of pillows in decreasing sizes, these were elaborately worked in coloured silks and metal threads on silk or satin, the overall background often having a quilted pattern. Baroque and chinoiserie exuberance was a studied feature of some and designs were frequently in the form of a central garland or motif with corresponding smaller ones at the four corners and a complex border around the edge. Baskets of flowers, or cornucopiae in chain-stitch and long-and-short flat stitches respectively, were favourite motifs. Many less elaborate examples were made by amateurs and beautiful ones survive. Monochrome examples, either professional or amateur, include one of gilt bullion with small coloured silk ovals at Drayton House, and another remarkable earlier one of exceptionally large proportions in rust coloured silk with a raised

Figure 63
Queen Anne bed coverlet, the cotton ground finely decorated with false quilting, and embroidered with coloured silks.

Plates 21 a & b
Two of the large tent stitch hangings from Stoke Edith, Herefordshire, depicting formal gardens and buildings, and worked in fine tent stitch.

Figure 64
Corner of a fine George I
coverlet with bright silk
and gold thread
embroidery and a false
quilted ground. *c.*1720.
(Full size 6 ft 8 in x 5 ft
11 in).

strapwork and foliate-design (*Plate 3a*). There is a very good collection of coverlets at Colonial Williamsburg. Ones of polychrome silks appear very graceful and delicate in contrast to the bold and woolly contemporary crewelwork (*Plate 3b*). The quilted background, false quilting, was essentially a decorative feature no longer forming a binding of warm layers of material. Professional quilters worked throughout the century for functional and decorative purposes, for furnishings and for costume. A number of patterns were used especially for decorative work. Rope-type twisted threads were sewn in lozenges, squares, roundels, hexagonal honeycomb form, and scale or scallop shell patterns. A wavy, vermicular line was another popular background pattern; it was known as Stormont, having been made fashionable by the whim of Lord Stormont. Quilting was usually done in yellow silks and occasionally overcouched with metal threads. Around the middle of the century much more elaborate patterns of flowers, leaves and feather designs were made, but not as a background for coloured embroidery.

Despite the apparent differences between crewel and silk bed furnishings in the first quarter of the 18th century, a number of common features can be noticed, such as tendrils of curling leaves, equally satisfactory when adapted to the refinement of silk. The veins of beautifully shaded leaves were often worked in red, a feature of oriental origin. Some coverlets were dotted with small chinoiserie motifs, related to the larger fantasies of wool embroidery.

Late-18th-century patchwork patterns were closely associated with quilting and were no doubt derived from them. Various pieces of fabric were cut and sewn in regular shapes, then applied on a backing in mozaic form giving a brilliant, stained glass, shimmering effect, often providing an interesting scrap-book collection of plain and printed materials. Patchwork was chiefly made for bed coverlets but sometimes also for hangings and occasionally garments, perhaps reminiscent of fools and harlequins. American patchwork was notable for a wide variety of designs, techniques and materials. At least 150 printed fabrics were used in one example, in addition to plain and woven materials. The country imported large quantities of printed cottons and even small off-cuts were saved for the purpose. However, American patchwork, as in Great Britain and Ireland, reached its peak at the beginning of the 19th century, so more will be said of it in the next chapter.

Knotting continued to be popular in the early 18th century, the threads being couched-down in crewelwork patterns for hangings,

Figure 65
Detail of an Irish linen coverlet of knotted and couched cord made by Mrs Delany in 1765.
(8 ft 4 in x 7 ft 11 in).

coverlets and for furniture. A bed-cover made by Mrs Delany of couched knotting on Irish linen has a design of formal flowers in a tight interlacing pattern, and was a birthday present to Thomas Sandford in 1765. Loose-knotted macramé fringes were fashionable for several decades.

A transition from the homely techniques of crewelwork developed in several ways through the century. The tent-stitch hangings from Hatton Garden were mentioned earlier (*page* 91). A large pair on canvas, with a carpet *en suite* (*Plate 23*) at Aston Hall, Birmingham, is signed by Mary Holte, aged sixty, and dated 1744. The hangings are chiefly floral but panels depict Holte family houses, Aston Hall and Brereton Hall.[3] A further series of ten tall wall panels worked by Lady Julia Calverly, dated 1717, is still preserved at her home, Wallington Hall, Northumberland. Pictorial hangings are represented by three at Castle Ashby, Northampton which incorporate thirteen pastoral panels, each within a border and under a *trompe l'oeil* curtain valance, while a magnificent large pair of pictorial hangings in fine tent-stitch, from Stoke Edith (*Plate 21*), now at Montacute House, Somerset, depict formal garden scenes with tidy precision:

We see the Marks of the Scissars upon every Plant and Bush.

The Spectator *1712*

Parterres, tulips, clipped yew trees, ponds and garden ornaments, a summer house and an orangery are shown. Figures and dogs on the pathways are thought to be slightly later additions. These glorious panels epitomise the charms of architecture, gardening and needlework of the Queen Anne period. In the professional field, tapestries still had an elder brother influence. A panel at Alnwick Castle is in the style of a Soho tapestry by Joshua Morris in fine stitches and depicting baskets of flowers, parrots and strapwork against a buff and yellow background.

A delightful hanging signed 'Anne Grant 1750' is at Monymusk, Aberdeenshire. It shows vases and pots of flowers under an arcade, with trees, and swags of flowers hanging above. Also in Scotland, at Wemyss Castle, Fife there is a set of four bed curtains worked by Janet, Lady Wemyss, dated 1727-30, with the initials of her children, as they were born, on each respective curtain. They are of fine linen, woven with blue satin, in broad vertical stripes, and are embroidered with small vases of flowers, delicately arranged. These are interspersed with small chinoiserie birds and sprigs. As was often the case, the patterns are largely repetitive but the colours are varied. The clear-cut stripes of blue and white might be thought to be more typical of a late-18th-century trend to simplify forms with plainer lines which ultimately led to a revival of Greek and Roman decorative principles, in neo-classicism.

Neo-classical needlework is fairly rare. Relatively little was made, probably because the technique did not lend itself especially well to the style. But two panels made to designs of the most important English exponent of neo-classicism, Robert Adam, at Newliston, Midlothian, are of interest. Neat formations of urns, sphynxes, and hanging baskets of flowers are depicted in felt appliqué, partly tinted with watercolour, on a yellow moiré woollen fabric. The hangings were made about 1792-5. Twelve others of the same set, in poor condition, were sold at Sotheby's in 1928. A bed with curtains in a similar technique from Newliston is at the National Trust for Scotland's house at 7 Charlotte Square, Edinburgh. All these were probably made by Lady Mary Hog. A large number of felt appliqué pictures were also made from about this time depicting birds, flowers, fruit (especially strawberries) and also more ambitious subjects. Fruits were often padded and suspended in three dimensional form.

Chinoiserie was a more frivolous and ubiquitous fashion, playing a part in both rococo and neo-classical tastes. Early in the century, Soho tapestries with dark blue and brown backgrounds, perhaps derived from lacquer, depicted isolated oriental vignettes, as imagined through European eyes. (*See Fig. 70.*) The subjects were treated with a certain quaintness and lack of distinction between Chinese, Persian or Indian figures, and with a charmed quality characteristic of the Chinese taste that pervaded art from the 17th to 19th centuries. The fantasies of 'China work' were associated with the extremes of rococo, in which naturalistic forms became exotic and fanciful. Both were exemplified in the furniture designs of Thomas Chippendale whose influential book *The Gentleman and Cabinet-Maker's Director* was published in 1754. Sir William Chamber's *Designs for Chinese Buildings* (1757) reflected the fascination of such projects, even if they were only temples of the air, and encouraged the fashion generally, inspiring even needlework.

Imported Chinese wallpaper and porcelain continued to be both direct and indirect sources of inspiration, as were lacquerwork designs, while yellow, the imperial colour of the Ching dynasty, became a favourite background colour for needlework. Chinoiserie scenes tended to be done in tight pictorial patches on an uncluttered background, within reserves, as in lacquer and porcelain, and were depicted in great detail. Other less obvious oriental forms were adopted such as elegant feathery leaves and blocks of in-filled trellis pattern—a criss-cross, with studs on the intersections. This was especially used on costume. Countless oriental birds, pheasants usually, rather than phoenixes, were intermingled with mythological, exotic and homely local species in charming harmony: '. . . birds praising Our Lord without discord, the popyngay, the mavys, partryge, pecocke, thrushe, nyghtyngale, larke, egle, dove, phenix, wren, the tyrtle trew, the hawke, the pelly cane, the swalowe, all singing in quaint blending of Latin and English the praises of God'. (As described in a pamphlet entitled *Wild Flowers and Birds as Seen on 18th Century Needlework*.) Real foreign birds were accurately embroidered in picture form, individually or in small groups, perhaps with a moth or

Figure 66
Part of a Piedmontese silk hanging with chinoiserie appliqué and embroidered birds and flowers. Italy *c.* 1765.

Figure 67
Canvaswork panel of featherlike leaves in reds, blues, greens and yellows on a dark blue background. Dated 1741.

two, in the manner of William Hayes' engravings or the embossed paper versions painted by Samuel Dixon.

Early-18th-century books were published with the intention of being useful for various purposes, gardening, painting and needlework and, conversely, designs were undoubtedly taken from many other sources. Pattern drawers still carried out individual commissions; Abraham Pinhorn, who was married in 1731, is known to have drawn 'all sorts of Patterns for Needlework, French Quilting, Embroidery, Cross and Tent Stitch'. He also supplied 'shades of silk and Worsted'. In 1732 Marmaduke Smith advertised 'an entirely new Collection of Patterns for Ladies' Work' including designs for chair seats, screens and carpets.

From about the middle of the century women went out to the American colonies to teach sewing of every kind including samplers, and to draw patterns and sell others and canvas. They advertised their services in local newspapers. In the *Boston Newsletter* of 1738 Mrs Condy offered: 'All sorts of beautiful Figures on Canvas, for Tent Stick; the Patterns from London, but drawn by her much cheaper than English drawing'. She supplied too: 'Silk Shades Slacks Floss Cruells of all Sorts, the best White Chapple Needles, and everything for all Sorts of Work'.

Beautiful needlework carpets were made in the 18th century, sometimes by professionals, but more often by amateurs. They were predominantly in designs of leaves and flowers (*Plates 23a & 24b*), though some of the earliest were of leaves only, in stylised form like crewelwork. Gradually they became more fluid with frayed, curling leaves, and a greater oriental feeling and more colour. Further varieties of foliage followed in smaller scale and with increasing numbers of flowers. Eventually a mass of larger or smaller blooms displaced the leaves and filled the whole design. Contrasts of pattern were maintained with a fairly deep border and a central panel, sometimes shaped as in oriental carpets. Some designs showed vases or baskets at the base from which sprang huge sprays of flowers. Backgrounds were of blue, red, cream, yellow, brown and purple. An unusual example recently acquired by the Metropolitan Museum has a variety of patterns, chiefly geometric, but also includes a text. It is dated 1764. Rococo, chinoiserie and Georgian Gothic designs of unrestricted, large sizes were all practised on carpets as overall patterns, or in pictorial forms. Table carpets usually had concentric designs around the border, though the central panel might lie in a horizontal plane.

From about 1760 geometric designs tended to replace floral patterns, being featured either in the border, or the main part, or as a background to flowers and leaves. Key patterns, octagonal bamboo patterns and trellis designs were also incorporated. The many variations were made as alternatives to the increasingly popular woven carpets produced at Kidderminster, Wilton, Kilmarnock and Axminster. Moorfields hand-knotted carpets were in demand during the second part of the century

and were especially favoured by Robert Adam. Few needlework carpets
were made in the neo-classical style; the technique and texture was
somewhat incompatible with the hard lines and smooth steely sheens
of the period. However, a good example worked to an Adam pattern
from Croome Court was recently seen in the salerooms, and the original
designs for this and others of its kind are in the British Museum and
Soane Museum, London.

English and French canvaswork was often virtually indistinguishable.
A set of four large hanging panels at the Musée Nissim de Camondo of

Figure 69
This large panel was made in about 1730 to record the discovery of a Roman pavement at Littlecote Park, Wiltshire, which was covered up again and rediscovered in 1978.

Figure 70
Charming absurdities of
chinoiserie on the back
of a mid-18th-century
French giltwood fauteuil.

*c.*1740 are very close in style to English carpets. Each panel shows a vase piled high with flowers, leaves, and with large bouquets above, on an off-white background, within a border of similar foliage on a blue background.

Many other sizeable needlework projects in finer tent stitch were undertaken which were of an ambitious and original nature. At Wallington Hall there is a black laquer six-fold screen signed by (Lady) Julia Calverly, 1727. It incorporates large panels depicting scenes adapted from an edition of Virgil's *Eclogues and Georgics* published by John Ogilvy in 1654, with illustrations by Francis Cleyn who was also a designer at the Mortlake tapestry factory. An unusual panel at Littlecote, Wiltshire of about 1730, depicts the Roman pavement that was discovered in the park but was subsequently reburied to avoid crowds of curious visitors. Very fine sewing delineates every detail of the archaeological remains which are now being excavated again. (*Fig. 69.*)

A large number of smaller canvas embroideries were carried out for the seats and backs of sets of chairs. Many were of a floral design, others pictorial, derived from illustrations, and some heraldic, as for a set of gilt furniture at Berkeley Castle, Gloucestershire. Further discussion of needlework for furniture is included towards the end of this book.

SAMPLERS

In the 17th century samplers were worked by teenage girls and adults but by the 18th century they were exclusively done by younger children. They were technically simpler and more decorative. Many, from around the middle of the century, show the age of the child and it is not surprising that they were not expected to use metal threads and do raised work as in the previous century. A few samplers were, however, done by older women, as examples for their children.

By about 1725 the usual shape of samplers was squarer and a variety of fabrics was used. Linen was the chief one, sometimes of a coarse weave and of a yellowish colour. Tammy, a fine wool cloth, became an alternative for a short period. Satin and tiffany (a fine glazed muslin material) were used for map and darning samplers. Threads of silk and linen were used. The old format of a large number of bands was replaced by wider ones of increased interest, more like pictures, and by the middle of the century wide borders are seen around a relatively small panel of lettering, texts and motifs. These borders were usually filled with delicate scrolling flowers of all colours, similar in style to some Queen Anne coverlets, and sometimes stemming from a basket at the base, perhaps resting on undulating hillocks. On other occasions there was a landscape scene at the bottom with shepherdesses, houses, trees, etc. Some girls, especially in America, were expected to do two sorts of sampler: firstly, a plain one of alphabets and numerals, which was good practice for the marking of linen, a normal task on entering into service

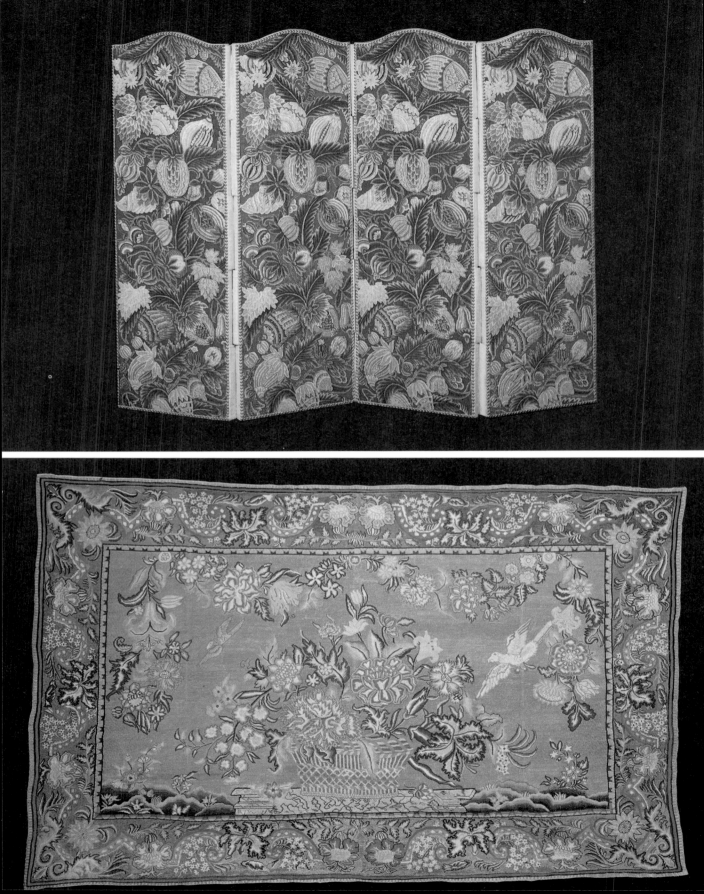

in a household; and secondly, a more decorative one to be regarded as a peak of sewing achievement. Middle-class families were justly proud of the charming little works that their children learned to do in schools and at home and many samplers were framed, glazed and hung on parlour walls. The sizes varied greatly as did the fineness of the stitching. Some large samplers were made, up to 30 in (76 cm) wide, and divided into sections with texts, patterns and animal motifs; but the sewing on these usually lacks the grace of smaller ones.

An unexpected form of sampler with an earlier lace-like appearance was that of holy-work or hollie-point. Always of white, these represented work done on baby clothes and caps. The name was derived from a needlepoint lace stitch of three centuries earlier. Patterns were made of small pin prick holes, being in fact gaps in a build-up of buttonhole stitching over an area where the fabric had previously been cut away. On samplers the technique is usually combined with whitework borders, drawn thread or cutwork. The designs were always simple, showing stylised flowers, an occasional bird or animal, and a number of crowns, hearts, a date and geometric patterns.

Other whitework samplers, or parts of samplers, included features derived from earlier Italian sources—cutwork (*reticello*), drawn thread work and needle lace including *punto in aria*.

As stylised bands gradually disappeared from 18th-century samplers they were replaced by pictorial motifs. Some of these were adapted from the spot samplers of the previous century but others of an angular nature also developed and soon became standard conventions. Adam and Eve under a fruit tree, boxers, crowns, stags and hearts had all featured before and continued to do so, while houses, other animals including dogs and sheep, and human figures were introduced together with a naturalistic portrayal of flowers. Seven year old E. Philips depicted her entire family in 1761 but on the whole the combination and composition of motifs was formal and conventional. The charm was in the workmanship. Occasionally, topical interest is reflected as in a sampler at Bethnal Green Museum signed 'Mary Hall. Wye 1786' which

Plate 24a (top)
One of a pair of Régence screens, each having four folds with a repeating design. French, *c*.1720. Height 5 ft 3½ in.

Plate 24b (bottom)
18th-century carpet of wool worked in cross stitch, the central panel framed within a border of flowers and strapwork. *c*.1740. 8 ft 4 in x 5 ft 6 in.

shows a hot air balloon rising from the ground, clearly alluding to the Montgolfier brothers.

The use of a continuous border pattern framing the main part of the sampler began around 1720; the zig-zag form enclosing flowers was derived from bands on 17th-century samplers. The vine-like chain is filled with single or alternating floral motifs, especially honeysuckle, but this became increasingly stylised and ultimately a rather weak convention. However, the awkward turning round corners betrays, charmingly, the child's difficulties.

Samplers taught not only sewing but also alphabets and numerals, in a variety of scripts. Sometimes several kinds are included in one sampler. John Brightland's *Grammar of the Englishe Tongue* (1711) contained an alphabet of 'sampler letters' and was much used as a pattern book. As they progressed, children were sometimes required to undertake lengthy texts in needlework and many examples can be seen of small lettering in fine stitching, usually in monochrome, red, black, green or blue, and surrounded by other motifs in several colours. The ten commandments (*Exodus*, Chapter 20) on two tablets were a favourite. An example in a private collection in red, green and blue is signed 'Jane Brain Iuly the 6th 1738'. The Lord's Prayer was similarly worked and short essays on virtues such as 'Meekness'. Another sampler has two poems 'Of Love' and 'Of Sincerity' worked in red on panels within a flower border and signed 'Sarah Maggee her work 1729'. Later examples, usually worked in black alone with no additional decorative features, spelled out painfully slowly, educative lessons such as 'Geography' (1797).[4]

Many samplers had shorter texts of four to eight lines, sometimes Bible quotations, but more often moral verses or proverbial sayings, of a puritanical and priggish tone. They were full of terrifying warnings of the imminence of death, pious persuasions to virtue, and self-righteous warnings against human temptations, adapted from writers such as the non-conformist churchman Dr Isaac Watts, author of *Divine and Moral Songs for Children* (1720). Morbid reminders of the shortness and uncertainty of life were indelibly stamped into tiny children's minds as they spent days slowly stitching them:

> Let not the Morrow your vain Thoughts employ
> But think this Day the last you may enjoy.

Poignant verses told the children that their lives were frail and transitory. It seems unnecessary that Mary Wakeling's otherwise charming sampler (Victoria and Albert Museum) of 1742, worked when she was ten, should have such a gloomy rhyme as this:

> Gay dainty flowers go swiftly to decay,
>   poor wretched life's short portion flies away,
> we eat, we drink, we sleep but lo, anon,
>   old age steals on us, never thought upon.

Some texts commemorated the feasts of Christmas, Easter and Ascensiontide. Though the Crucifixion appeared on samplers from continental Europe, particularly in Germany, it was not common on English ones. Occasionally special prayers were embroidered; some were simple and pious, but others were ridiculously trite:

Figure 71
Sampler with an unusual border and well-balanced design, signed 'Martha Grundy her work in the eleventh year of her Age 1766'.

Oh may thy powerful word
Inspire a breathing worm
To rush into thy Kingdom Lord
And take it as by storm.

Samplers were even used to drum into children the dangers of thoughts of love, and other aspects of evil imagination. Elizabeth Bock, in 1764, was made to sew into her work:

And if I should by a young youth be
Tempted
Grant I his schemes defy and all
He has invented.

Proverbial texts were more reasonable and, displayed on the wall, provided for periodic reflection:

Be not hasty in thy spirit to be angry: for anger resteth in the
bosom of fools.

Sarah Grimes' text of 1730 is a little prim but none the less a sensible and neatly composed nursery tract:

Keep a strict guard over thy tongue, thine ear and thine eye, lest
they betray thee to talk things vain and unlawful. Be sparing of
thy words, and talk not impertinently or in passion. Keep the
parts of thy body in a just decorum, and avoid immoderate
laughter and levity of behaviour.[5]

This must indeed have drawn her attention not only to bodily care but also to long words she had never considered before. A fascinating sampler by Mary Dudden of Cardiff, 1780, is a moral lesson of Langland or Bunyan complexity, enough to keep the sewer thinking for a lifetime:

THE LIFE OF HAPPY MAN

The happy Man was born in the city of Regeneration, in the
Parish of Repentance unto Life, was educated at the School of
Obedience, and now lives in the Plain of Perseverance, he works
at the Trade of Diligence, not withstanding he has a large Estate
in the County of Christian Contentment and many Times does
Jobs of Self-denial.

A note attached to the back board of the sampler informs us: 'Mary Dudden were 12 years of age when this sampler were worked, and some part of it by moonlight'. Some texts were in the form of acrostics, where the initial letters of each line spelled out a word or name. A pleasant verse of 'Anno Dom: 1749' in this form is

A   virgin that's Industrious, Merits Praise,
N   ature she Imitates in Various Ways,
N   ow forms the Pink, now gives the Rose its blaze.

Y oung Buds, she folds, in tender Leaves of green,
O mits no shade to beautify her Scene.
U pon the Canvas, see, the Letters rise,
N eatly they shine with intermingled dies,
G lide into Words, and strike us with Surprize.

Other samplers were worked in the form of a Rebus, some words being replaced by pictograph vignettes. Perpetual almanacs in table form, and genealogical charts showing family birth dates were also made towards the end of the century, usually in black with little coloured ornament.

Map samplers, combining experience in sewing with Geography, were popular in the last two or three decades of the century. Sometimes they were drawn out individually and on other occasions they were worked over printed patterns. The sewer often marked her own native village prominently amongst the familiar landmarks. Great Britain and Europe were frequent subjects as were single and double hemispheres also. Individual maps of Ireland and countries far afield perhaps indicate personal connections; they often show quaintly inaccurate or unknown boundaries and territories, as for example in Canada and large parts of America. Australia was often marked 'New Holland'. A map of Africa dated 1784 'Done at Mrs. Arnold's Fetherston Buildings' shows markings such as Grain Coast, Tooth Coast and Slave Coast alongside the more familiar Gold Coast.[6]

English darning samplers are of special charm and were probably inspired by Dutch originals. Earlier ones consisted of adjoining squares of fairly coarse darning patterns while others were of finely worked vertical crosses of darning scattered over an area. Both were worked in a variety of coloured silks, sometimes with additional decorative motifs including flowers and birds. A popular format consisted of a posy of flowers tied with a ribbon with crosses of plain and coloured darning alongside, surrounded by a border of intertwined flowers. (*Plate 25c*)

Some very individual and rare samplers include a beadwork one by 'Jane Millf', about 1760, showing spot motifs including many birds, trees, vases of flowers and squirrels. Another interesting curiosity is a diminutive sampler of only $5\frac{1}{2}$ in x 5 in (14 cm x $12\frac{1}{2}$ cm). It is very finely worked with a verse and motifs, including cats on cushions, Adam and Eve under a tree with the snake, and baskets of flowers, all within a conventional border pattern.

The tradition of sampler making was naturally taken to North America but 18th-century examples made in that country, of which a large number have been preserved, were significantly independent in style. Unlike their European counterparts, they were primarily decorative, and instead of having the characteristic angular features, were densely covered with naturalistic, flowing embroidery, more like needlework pictures. Pictorial subjects often filled part of the canvas and sometimes the entire background was worked over. The depiction

Plate 25a (top left)
A sampler with alphabets and a floral border, signed 'Hannah Trampten 1752'.

Plate 25b (top right)
A conventional but finely worked sampler by 'Mary Lovejoy, 1808'.

Plate 25c (bottom)
Late-18th-century darning sampler, dated 1788. English or Dutch. (Detail).

of foliage was not stylised as in England and the conventional border
patterns were not common. Texts were less prominent but a border of
flowers often framed a central panel in which were lettering, a scene with
a house, a church, figures, animals, trees, etc. Human figures were
depicted and also two specially American hallmarks, the eagle and
weeping willows. So many good samplers have survived that some can
be identified in groups or even as the work of particular schools, or as
made under the direction of a specific teacher. Samplers done by girls
in schools in Pennsylvania often have a border within a border and a
picture in the centre, neo-classical in feeling, showing a doleful and high-
waisted lady standing under a willow tree. A group from Providence,
Rhode Island, supervised by a teacher called Mary Balch, often portray a
public building in considerable detail. A pair of pillars flank the main
panel of the sampler, and outside this is a floral border. The background
canvas was frequently totally filled in with stitching. Samplers from
Salem, Massachusetts, worked at Miss Sarah Stivour's school show the
distinctive use of a long stitch of crinkled silk for backgrounds. They
also have a landscape at the bottom.

Samplers from continental Europe were less decorative than English or American ones but often technically superior, with a greater variety of stitches and colour combinations. They were less pictorial, more a collection of patterns and of a less personal nature, usually without texts and not showing the age of the sewer. French ones were nearest in form to the English but often more tightly filled with motifs. Spain, Portugal, Italy, Switzerland and Holland all produced samplers. Denmark was renowned for fine whitework and this was reflected in her samplers. An example dated 1758 (Victoria and Albert Museum) shows no less than ninety-eight neat squares of varying drawn thread and embroidered patterns. Dutch samplers were broad rather than long with patterns worked horizontally, and consisted of a fairly haphazard collection of motifs without formal composition. Spanish samplers show densely packed rows of intricately worked border patterns, sometimes with an heraldic device in the middle. They were not usually dated. Alphabets were not used much. German ones, on the other hand, were often made up of alphabets and numerals only, usually in red. I have seen one with continuous rows of alphabets in nineteen different scripts, with numerals also and two tidy columns of border bands. Other German samplers show a Crucifixion motif with the instruments, such as ladder, nails, scourge, hammer, sponge, hour-glass, dice, cock and the crown of thorns. Adam and Eve, wild animals and exotic birds were amongst other motifs. The arrangement of these symbols had a certain unity but never had the decorative form so characteristic of American samplers. Some English ones were also devised almost as pictures with a signature squeezed in at the top or bottom. A delightful example shows principally a large basket of flowers resting on hillocky ground. Above it is a saying from Proverbs and below: 'Ann Stibbs Workt This Piece Of Work At Mrs Rea Bording School Tower Hill, London Finisht Iune the 25 1754'. It is not surprising that details are given in full since needlework was taken very seriously and the art and pleasure of it were frequently a lady's chief accomplishment and interest. From childhood, the skill required was linked with the morals, discipline and hopes provided by religion:

> Jesus permit thy gracious name to stand,
> As the first effort of an infants hand,
> And while her fingers on the canvas move,
> Engage her tender thoughts to seek thy love,
> With thy dear children let her have A part,
> And write thy name thyself upon her heart.

Though it had to be expressed in terms of relative humility, the inference is that needlework was second only to godliness—(Mary Cole, 1759):

> Better by far for Me
> Than all the Simpster's Art
> That God's commandment be
> Embroidered on my heart.

LATER FASHIONS IN COSTUME, FURNISHINGS AND PICTURES

By the middle of the 18th century male and female costume was gloriously decorative and embroidery at the zenith of fashion; a considerable industry based at Lyons generated and co-ordinated influences and dispensed products to the high societies of many European countries. In England professional artists, designers and embroiderers supplied the main corpus of decorative coats, waistcoats and dresses but some of the finest specimens were home produced. Mrs Delany was an archetype of the period and its tastes and, having been born in 1700, even her age coincided with the years of the century. She was twice married, lived at Glasnevin, near Dublin, and in London and Windsor. She knew the King and Queen and many celebrities of the day, and was a diarist and accomplished practiser of a variety of domestic arts including needlework. Lady Llanover described a petticoat of Mrs Delany's as:

> covered with sprays of natural flowers, in different positions, including the burgloss, auriculas, honeysuckle, wild roses, lilies of the valley, yellow and white jessamine, interspersed with small single flowers. The border at the bottom being entirely composed of large flowers in the manner in which they grow, both *garden* and *wild* flowers being intermingled where the form, proportions and foliage rendered it desirable for the effect of the whole.

Mrs Delany was a keen gardener and clearly enjoyed both cultivated and natural beauty. She also recorded details of the individual tastes of celebrated contemporaries.

> The Duchess of Queensberry's clothes pleased me best. They were white satin embroidered, the bottom of the petticoat *brown hills* covered with all sorts of weeds, and every breadth had an *old stump of a tree* that ran up almost to the top of the petticoat, broken and ragged, and worked with brown chenille, round which were twined nastertiums, ivy, honeysuckles, periwinkles, convolvuluses, and all sorts of twining flowers, which spread and covered the petticoat.

This same Duchess did not however please that princeling of taste in Bath, Beau Nash, when she wore an embroidered apron at the Assembly Rooms. He tore it off her, but she reacted in good humour apparently, despite the fact that the garment was of fine needlepoint lace, and said to have cost 500 guineas. An earlier apron at Nottingham Museum of Costume, signed and dated 'EW 1721' is of fine whitework with exotic oriental birds and flowers. Short decorative aprons had been introduced to England from France where they were worn in the late 17th century. They derived from a passion amongst pampered court ladies for pretending to be dairy maids. But the English ones were of heavy silk in plain rectangular form or with a scalloped lower edge. Some had

Plate 26
The underside of the canopy of a fine silk bed made for Queen Charlotte to a design by Robert Adam.

pockets, and others were trimmed with lace or gold lace. They were either delicately embroidered with light porcelain-like flower sprigs or were heavily embroidered with metal threads and colourful vases, baskets or cornucopiae of flowers. Flowing chinoiseries and other exotic fantasies provided further variations. An alternative type of apron was of fine muslin, decorated with traditional whitework, or tambour embroidery.[7]

The old skill of tambouring was brought from China to France in about 1760 where it quickly became fashionable. Even Madame de Pompadour was painted doing it. The technique involved sewing with a hook onto material stretched on a hoop (*tambour* meaning *drum*). The ground material was usually cream silk or satin and the relatively fast stitching was very fine. The most popular subjects were those typical of Louis XVI's reign—architectural remains such as broken classical columns, rustic figures, birds, butterflies, fruit and flowers and groups of musical instruments with tambourines and scores. The bright silks have invariably faded to soft ochres and greens.[8]

The Louis XVI style was the first major part of a wave of neo-classicism that was heralded across Europe as a kind of second Renaissance. Following excavations at Pompeii and other Roman sites, a sense of

Figure 73
Louis XVI panel, chiefly worked in tambour embroidery. French *c.* 1775.

new learning led to widespread remodelling of architecture and decoration and a new intellectual taste. Urns, and swags of husks and sphynxes were incorporated with classical pediments and columns to the exclusion of previous fashions. But the new vogue did not combine naturally with the techniques of needlework, as mentioned earlier, and as a result the craft was less used with a preference for plain or striped silks. Neo-classicism was more noticeable in costume than in other forms of sewing. Hepplewhite and Sheraton furniture had light elegant lines that called for plain or simple coverings rather than the fussy ornament of embroidery. Needlewomen therefore turned their attention once again away from practical works to incidental decorative pictures. They did not attempt anything too serious but were content to sew lightweight designs in keeping with the semi-academic mood of the times. Pictures depicting oriental pheasants had much in common with porcelain painting, for example first period Worcester, but many subjects were derived from prints and worked in fine silks that resembled engravings and even imitated them in certain cases. Pretty and female, they lacked the originality or forthrightness of earlier needlework, though in fact they frequently portrayed similar subjects. Seventeenth-century themes, such as Old Testament stories, together with familiar tales from the classics and mythology, were retold in sentimental renderings of silk, and closely followed the mezzotints of Francesco Bartolozzi (1727–1815), Angelica Kauffman (1741–1807) and others. The paintings of Wheatley and Cipriani were alternative sources with a similar stamp of mellow gracefulness, often in an oval format. Details of faces and hands

Figure 74
Silk and chenille picture of a family on a terrace, the garden gate with the monogram 'CL'. French or Swiss, *c.*1925. (20¾ in x 16 in).

were painted and sometimes much of the backgrounds, the sewers having given in to Mrs Delany's understandable complaint: 'It is provoking to have the ground take up so much more time than the flowers'. The painting of faces had an old precedent for this was done in mediaeval embroidery (e.g. an early-14th-century altar frontal at Château-Thierry). Chenille was used for some parts especially in pastoral scenes where it was appropriate for sheep and trees. Often a sense of delightful melancholy prevailed in these pictures. 'Fame Strewing Flowers on Shakespeare's Tomb' was a particularly popular subject, embroidered countless times with little originality. Symbols of mourning, derived from Greek and Roman models, provided 'a reflection on decayed magnificence'[9]—urns, tombs, follies, sylvan glades with Flora, Bacchus and other gods and classical figures beside ruined temples and grottos. Religious pictures also included New Testament scenes such as the Resurrection, Christ and Mary Magdalene, and Christ with the lady at the well. Romantic literary themes were popular too, illustrations of subjects from Goethe being a favourite.

Monochrome pictures, sometimes in hair but more often in black silks with some lighter shades, had a sober smartness. Worked on silk or satin, these imitated engravings, etchings and drawings have been termed 'printwork'. Usually on a larger scale than the polychrome silk pictures, they depicted imaginary or real topographical subjects such as Burghley House. Occasionally they were signed, as were versions after engravings of Cambridge colleges by Lamborn, e.g. one showing the Wren library and the river at Trinity College, 'H.B. Wells. '89'. Smaller rustic landscapes in a similar technique followed in the 19th century.

Late 18th-century American pictures differed slightly in spirit,

Figure 75
Black silk and hair 'printwork' picture of Burghley House, Northamptonshire, *c.*1785.

often having a certain studied naivety. Designs included landscapes, pastoral scenes, views of architecture and ships, maps, portraits, biblical and mythological subjects, memorials, flower pieces and allegorical compositions. Some commemorated George Washington. They were embroidered with a variety of stitches in floss or twisted silks. As in England, the sky and faces were usually painted and they were often given a black glass mount with a gilt frame, very much a feature of Regency taste.

Sentimental but fine quality pictures were worked in schools. The Moravians founded two institutions in Bethlehem, near Philadelphia in 1749 and here girls were taught the silk-work that made these pictures fashionable. In addition they made banners, including a surviving example from the American Revolution, known as the Pulaski Banner, that now belongs to the Maryland Historical Society, Baltimore. Some thirty-six panels in tent stitch from New England are generically termed the Fishing Lady pictures in reference to a central motif. They were closely based on contemporary prints. Other embroidery pictures generally had an atmosphere of melancholy gloom with titles like *The First, Second and Last Scene of Mortality*, an example worked by Prudence Punderson *c.*1775 (Connecticut Historical Society, Hartford).

Larger imitations of oil paintings in wool embroidery were a new development which was immensely admired following the successes of several professional and semi-professional embroideresses. In 1771 Arthur Young described in great detail needlepaintings after old masters by Miss Morret of Rokeby, Yorkshire. They included two Zuccarelli landscapes, two Gaspar Poussin landscapes, an unfinished picture after Rubens, and a picture by Salvator Rosa entitled *Democritus in a Contemplative Mood*. Mary Knowles (1733–1807) was a friend of Dr Johnson and herself a noted conversationalist. She too was famed for elaborate needlework copies of paintings. Queen Charlotte commissioned her to copy Zoffany's portrait of George III (Victoria and Albert Museum) and another large-scale embroidered picture commemorates the event, showing Mrs Knowles working the portrait (Kew Palace). Mary Linwood (1756–1845) exhibited similar works, with great success, at permanent displays in London and also in Edinburgh and Dublin. At Hanover Square in 1798 she showed a hundred copies after artists such as Raphael and Rubens, and many other painters and portraitists of the period from continental Europe and England. Her exhibitions became a social phenomenon like Madame Tussaud's wax models, though the popularity did not last in the same way. A London guidebook describing the pictures concluded: '. . . in a word, Miss Linwood's exhibition is one of the most beautiful the metropolis can boast and should unquestionably be witnessed, as it deserves to be, by every admirer of art'. She laid out her shows with the greatest theatrical panache, even with gas lighting, an enterprising novelty in those days, so that viewing could continue through winter afternoons. A Stubbs lioness appeared to be nothing short of the real creature emerging from a cave. She also delighted in narrative subjects such as James Northcote's *Lady Jane Grey visited by the Abbot and Keeper of the Tower by Night*. Miss Linwood was generally celebrated and was received by the Royal Family, the Empress of Russia, the King of Poland and Napoleon, whose portrait she embroidered twice. She left what she considered her masterpiece, a picture after Carlo Dolci, *Salvator Mundi* to Queen Victoria. Other works are now at the Museum of Leicester, her birthplace.[10] These include a large scene showing a woodman and a dog, after a lost painting by Thomas Gainsborough.

Figure 77
Eighteenth-century needlepainting—a large sewn version by Mrs Linwood of Gainsborough's *Woodman in a Storm*, now lost. (8 ft x 5 ft 6 in.)

Whitework embroidery was continuously made since its origin in lace costume accessories. Denmark was especially famed for it, on fine lawn, a semi-transparent linen, with linen thread or imported cotton. Hedebo and Amager embroidery was renowned, combining floral decoration and drawn-thread work, on locally woven grounds. But it was in Scotland that 'sewed muslin' whitework grew to become an important industry at the end of the 18th century. It became known as 'Ayrshire' embroidery, though the first design workshops and businesses were centred around Edinburgh. An Italian, Luigi Ruffini, set up a workshop in 1782 and successive ventures led to a massive production of whitework in the 19th century. Agents co-ordinated the manufacture of intricately embroidered christening robes, caps, dresses and cuffs by women in their own homes and in factories. Several mechanical developments led to groups working together. Designs included imitations of French lace which was difficult to procure during the Napoleonic wars. The American Civil War threatened the supply of cotton but gradually the agents built up a thriving industry. They began exporting products to Europe in a needlework trade of an importance that had not been enjoyed since the production of *opus anglicanum* in the 14th century.

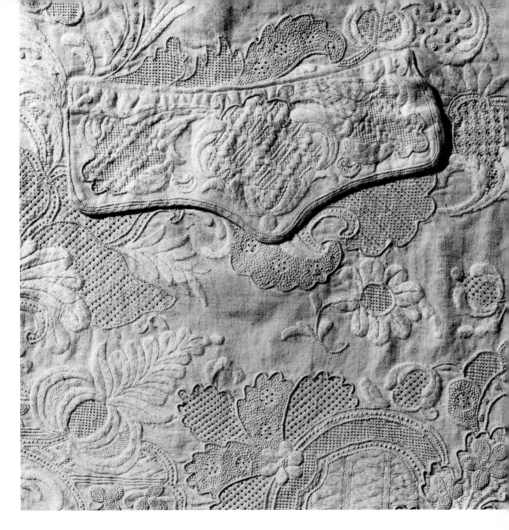

Figure 78
Detail of a man's white-
work waistcoat of
cotton and linen, *c*.1725.

NOTES

Epigram: W. Cooper, *The Task*, 1784.

1 *Country Life*, January 22nd, 1976. Michael Archer, 'Pyramids and Pagodas for Flowers'.

2 *Apollo* (date unknown) Margaret H. Swain, 'The Mellerstain Panel'.

3 The carpet, though similar, was probably made professionally and somewhat later. Another remarkable achievement may be noted, a set of bed hangings, six chairs, a carpet and window curtains made by Mrs Jennens, *c*.1731, for the Great Parlour Chamber at Weston Hall, Northamptonshire. Partly illustrated in *Country Life* January 22nd, 1976 in an article on the house by Francis Barnford.

4 Christie's, South Kensington, 4th December, 1979. Lot 61.

5 Quoted by Anne Sebba, *Samplers*, 1979.

6 Illustrated by Huish, op. cit.

7 There is a group of five aprons at Dyrham Park, Avon.

8 See for example a finely worked sofa cover at Waddesdon Manor, Buckinghamshire.

9 William Shenstone.

10 Several other wool-embroidered pictures are to be seen at Kew Palace.

6 The Nineteenth Century

Sad sewers make sad Samplers. We'll be sorry
Down to our fingers'-ends and 'broider emblems
Native to desolation—cypress sprays,
Yew tufts and hectic leaves of various autumn
And bitter tawny rue, and bent blackthorns.

REGENCY ENGLAND and Napoleonic France shared in their arts a general formal stamp of an Etruscan or Egyptian style. This was derived from the refined and academic neo-classicism of the late 18th century but it had a new intensity and hardness and was partly inspired by reports of motifs and emblems seen by military campaigners in North Africa. Architecture and interior decoration were subjected to the vogue but, on the whole, needlework was unsuited to the style, and surviving pieces in the manner are rare. Plain fabrics and materials with stripe weaves or small motifs, such as laurel crowns or Napoleonic bees, were more generally used.

Despite these fashionable innovations however, conventional forms, following those of the 18th century, continued to develop simultaneously in less elevated circles. Pictures in silks and wools were enormously popular, becoming increasingly stereotyped and less skilled in workmanship. The rise of a relatively prosperous middle class with a desire to emulate the comforts and cultural activities of their superiors led to a sudden expansion in embroidery which was no longer the preserve of privileged ladies. Needlework indeed became a general, and somewhat standardised, hobby with sizeable business repercussions. Large-scale, colourful 'fancy' embroidery of coarse, simple workmanship was produced in unrestrained quantities. The plain sewing of clothes was usually a morning occupation, while coloured work was done in the evenings, on Sundays and at times of social visiting. Tatting, a form of knotted work, continued to be a pastime. Jane Austen in a letter to her sister, Cassandra, in January 1809 wrote of her father: 'His working a footstool for Chawton is a most agreeable surprise to me . . . I long to know what his colours are—I guess greens and purples'.

Mary Linwood's needlework copies of contemporary oil paintings encouraged many amateurs to attempt pictures on a smaller scale. These were usually in wools in long and short stitches, but many varieties were tried out. Two examples by Lady Danesfort, in the Victoria and Albert Museum, depicting *Chichester Cathedral* (after Turner) and *The*

Plate 27a (top)
Early-19th-century silk picture depicting Christ's meeting with Mary Magdalene in the garden. The faces and sky are painted.

Plate 27b (bottom)
A woolwork picture, with painted faces, probably after an engraving of a painting by George Morland, *c.*1830.

Avenue (after Hobbema) are worked in tiny tent-stitch. Almost any canvas was considered for reproduction in needlepainting. George Morland and Francis Wheatley were frequently copied with the sentimental appeal of children and farmyard pets. As in silk pictures, the faces were often painted. Religious subjects were an alternative, frequently following an old master style. Silk 'printwork' embroidery was established in the previous century, and done in black, brown, cream and white silks, sometimes wholly, or partly, with hair. The pictures became smaller, often in an oval format and took on the appearance of etchings. F. V. Tanner, from Switzerland, exhibited examples of 'etching' embroidery at the Great Exhibition in 1851 and boosted interest in the technique.

Before considering specific developments of 19th-century needlework, a look at the samplers of the period will indicate some trends effecting changes in the basic conventions established in the 18th century.

SAMPLERS

Fine stitchery was no longer an essential part of a child's education and, unlike the practice in the two previous centuries, was certainly no longer required for creative needlweork. Latterly, however, there was a considerable interest in techniques, encouraged by a weariness of stagnant designs. This culminated in, for example, the popularity of Thérèse de Dillmont's *Encyclopaedia of Needlework* (English edition 1870).

Nineteenth-century samplers were fairly stereotyped; in many cases the dull, sad products of schools or nursery classes, they often recorded the misery that went into their making. But some were clearly done contentedly and proudly, and a few show considerable originality, breaking away from standard conventions. An example (*Fig. 82*) measuring 26 in long by 22 in wide (66 cm x 56 cm) shows, in a number of panels, flocks of sheep, horses, black swans, sailing ships and human figures as well as alphabets, a text and an extraordinarily large vase of

Figure 79
Woolwork picture of the Holy Family in the style of an old master painting. The faces, hands and background are painted. (Detail.)

Figure 80
A pair of small oval pictures, of black and pale brown silks, resembling etchings, *c*.1850. (7½ in long).

flowers.[1] Most samplers however were made up of a limited variety of alphabets, motifs, texts and borders, some with ridiculous rather than endearingly disproportionate scale relationships. A huge bird perching on a house was commonplace; human and animal figures in stylised, angular stitching often appear repetitive caricatures. However, a fair number of charming, decorative and even, at times, amusing samplers are well worth examination.

Children were sometimes required to attempt several kinds and an interesting series worked by Elizabeth Gardner of Glasgow (born 1806) indicates her progress. At the age of twelve she did one in worsteds, and two years later completed one in silks. In 1821, the following year, she did a most unusual one of drawn fabric as used for Dresden work. Finally, in 1822, aged sixteen, she completed a white sampler with squares in blue ribbon bands, a hollie-point centre, darning patterns and needlepoint lace fillings.

Many 19th-century samplers had no alphabets or numerals, nor even a name or date, but consisted solely of either symmetrical or random motifs spaced regularly over the linen canvas. The motifs were considerably more varied than in the previous century and increasingly included small, shaded vignettes in the romantic mood of the full-scale Berlin pictures, to be discussed shortly. Little scenes of ruins, children and pet animals, derived from engravings, depicted in naturalistic shades with faded backgrounds, are often seen. Shading had been used in 17th-century spot motifs but was entirely absent in 18th-century samplers.

A large sampler at Bethnal Green Museum by 'Elizabeth S. Musto Age 14' shows a fine scrapbook composition of characteristic subjects. A largish pastoral scene is flanked by two smaller views with an elegant gentleman and lady and a dog in a garden setting. A conventional border pattern encloses a poem and dozens of small motifs including a lion, an elephant, a tiger, a goat, a fox, a parrot, a peacock, shells, red ensign flags, a horn, a sword, a parasol, a boat, a gun, a key, a caduceus staff, rabbits, butterflies, books, scales, scissors, fighting cocks, a candle and fruit. The combination is typical of the haphazard selection of emblems chosen for semi-decorative, semi-educational purposes. Sometimes the outside zig-zag floral border was replaced by a Greek key pattern, a characteristic element of Regency decoration.

Many samplers were worked in classes at schools and orphanages. Some similar ones, reflecting varying ability, have survived together, perhaps because they were the work of sisters. Others show the names of class mates or friends, listed in differing colours, and a good many record the name of the school in a signature, e.g.: 'Worked at Mrs Ertights School by Mary Morgan April the 15 1805'. Many institutional samplers were notably of a practical rather than ornamental nature and were worked with great precision in preparation for tasks to be done when the girl entered into service. Rows of red or black alphabets in many scripts, sizes and numerals were practised. Border patterns and a few corner patterns, roundels and stars were perhaps combined with other small motifs. An individual type of sampler is associated with pupils of the Quaker Friends' school at Ackworth, and characterised by monochrome or polychrome wreaths, circles and octagons containing sprigs of flowers or initials. Mary Gregory's of 1807 was entirely of brown silks, made up of a combination of these fairly large geometrical forms. Other school samplers attempted to teach multiplication, money and calculation tables as well as incorporating useful perpetual almanacs. But the main educational message was invariably contained in a moral verse:

Figure 82
Corner of an unusual sampler, dated 1821, with flocks of sheep, horses, dogs, deer as well as ships and other motifs. 'Mary Faith, Aged 9'. (26 in x 22 in).

130

Figure 83
Sampler by 'Mary Snowden, Aged 8 Years' depicting the 'Queen's Palace', being either the Queen's House, Greenwich or Buckingham Palace before alterations.

While you my dear your needlework attend
Observe the counsel of a faithful friend
And strive an inward ornament to gain
Or all your needlework will prove in vain.

Ellen Shepherd Kesgrave School 1856.

Many were grim and morbid with solemn texts emphasising the horrors of hell, original sin, purgatory, rotting of bones, the jaws of death and the prospect of being suddenly thrown into an unknown world. Moreover the texts took a long time to do enabling the content to be soundly assimilated:

When I was young
And in my prime
Here you may see
How I spent my time.

The sewer often wept bitterly over her endless task but even this was regarded as morally strengthening:

> Patience will wipe away the streaming tear
> And hope will paint the pallid cheek of fear.

An otherwise charming and fine sampler at the Welsh Folk Museum, St Fagan's, signed 'Margaret Morgan Aged 14 Years 1839. S. Westbrook's School' contains Isaac Watt's terrifying saw, typical of many others:

> There is an hour when I must die.
> Nor can I tell how soon twill come.
> A thousand children young as I.
> Are calld by death to hear their doom.

On other occasions, however, the sewer got away with shorter and happier epithets such as: 'Home Sweet Home, be it ever so humble, there's no place like home'. This particular one was used, ironically, on samplers worked in an orphanage at Bristol.

Other samplers, as earlier, consisted of colossal texts, without decoration, of an instructive nature. The three Brontë sisters in 1829 and 1830 embroidered long passages from Proverbs in green-black silks, within a plain key pattern border. These historic but otherwise dull works still survive.[2]

Other kinds of sampler making, already practised in the 18th century, such as maps, continued with little change; acrostics and family records were also made. The former showed a verse, the initial letters of each line spelling out a name or 'Christ', etc., while the latter showed members of a family, alive and dead, in coloured and black threads. They were sometimes in the form of a family tree issuing at the root from heart-shaped plaques bearing the names of the parents. These were done especially in America. However, American samplers were generally not as elaborate as previously, less in the manner of embroidered pictures and often relatively simple. The Quaker schools for example taught a plainer form, often oval, with an uncomplicated vine leaf border.

Berlin woolwork samplers in a new format were done on long ribbons of canvas about 5–8 in wide (13–20 cm) and of various lengths, up to as much as 16 ft (4.9 m). Kept rolled up in the sewing box, they were close to the original purpose of samplers being true records of patterns, techniques and colour combinations for easy reference. They were not popularised as an achievement in themselves since they were neither decorative nor easy to display, but they had a certain charm, being embroidered with ingenious variety, colour, shading and frequently random spot motifs. A remarkable hanging known as the Dowell-Simpson sampler consists of a large number of 'visitor's book' pieces of a similar form, made between 1848 and 1896. The total size is 41 ft long by 18 in high (12½ m x 46 cm). The Berlin embroidery illus-

Figure 84
Family Sampler recording births and deaths. Signed 'Jane Howard Aged 13 1830'. (25 in x 16 in).

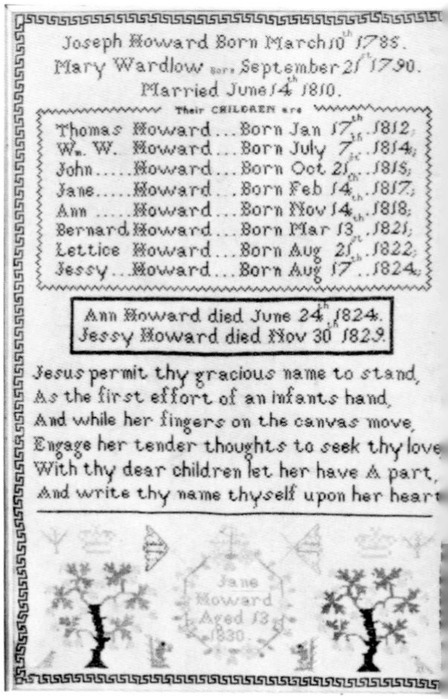

132

trates a large number of patterns and motifs, some of them of topical interest, and the introduction of 'gas colours', the bright synthetic aniline dyes which were developed around 1860.

Some children, in learning basic sewing, were taught to make miniature garments with a wide variety of stitching and seaming. These charming little apprentice pieces were kept together in albums for reference. They were remarkable technically and utterly different in quality from the coarse wool samplers so proudly framed and hung on parents' walls.

BERLIN WOOLWORK

Queen Victoria's reign, beginning in 1837, spanned two thirds of the 19th century and her name is rightly associated with all the vicissitudes of imperial expansion, and the achievements and shortcomings of a long and varied period.

A feature of art in the early part was an interest in romantic, mediaeval subjects, *le style troubadour*, incorporating castles, ruins, chivalry and all the 'stage' scenery of Sir Walter Scott's heroic novels. This was at the heart of the phenomenon of Berlin woolwork which enjoyed a colossal vogue from the 1830s for half a century. The craze appealed to the growing number of women who had time and money to spend on sewing; simple patterns and kits for doing it became a social appendage even to be carried around on visits to each other's houses. A picture of Florence Nightingale with her sister by W. White in the National

Portrait Gallery, London, shows her doing this kind of needlework. At a tea party at Brighton at which King William IV and Queen Adelaide were present, it was reported that the Queen sewed with the other ladies, and M. T. Morrall in *A History of Needlework* (1852) observed:

> If any lady comes to tea, her bag is first surveyed,
> And if the pattern pleases her, a copy there is made.

With the simple technique of working soft-coloured wools to squared patterns in plain tent- or cross-stitch, often with coarse threads, Berlin work displaced almost every other form of sewing. It alone became virtually synonymous with the word needlework; Mrs Henry Owen started *The Illuminated Book of Needlework* (1847) with the words: 'Embroidery, or as it is more often called Berlin wool-work . . .' Originally the technique was done in silks on fine mesh canvas for smallish items such as firescreens or a pair of face screens, as in the Museum of Costume in Bath, made by Queen Victoria for the Duchess of St Albans.

Figure 87
Part of a wool and silk panel for a firescreen. The background is silk canvas left unworked, *c.* 1850. (25 in x 19½ in).

It was made for accessory objects, including purses and bags. But wool as an alternative to silk on a coarser canvas was soon more general, and being easier to work and fairly inexpensive, was soon more favoured. By 1840 some fourteen thousand designs were in use, printed and then hand-coloured by armies of women earning pin money in publishers' warehouses. At least 1,200 were employed by the larger companies alone. The chief outlet was a shop in Regent Street, London where a Mr Wilks sold his imported patterns and bright 'Zephyr' or Berlin wools. The original designs were issued by a print seller in Berlin with hand-coloured shading, and overprinted with stitch squares, both appealing innovations. Merino wool from Saxony was spun in Gotha, dyed in Berlin and exported. Later, wools were produced in England, Scotland and France. Several kinds of canvas were used; silk canvas of a fine mesh was usually left partially unsewn. It was made of silk-bound cotton and was available in several colours, but as it was not suitable for wear, it was limited to pictures, fire screen panels, table screens, banners and bell-pulls. Jute canvas was tough for cushions, carpets, upholstery and heavy pelmets. Cotton, woollen, Java and Double (or Penelope) canvases were also used, of various degrees of coarseness. Designs were highlighted with silks and use was made of silk chenille in two thicknesses. Glass beads from France added lustre, and were sometimes used extensively in mixed or single colours; the weight of them helped banners to hang well. Bugles (long pipe-shaped beads), metal beads and pearls were also used, but less frequently. Plush-stitch raised work provided further variety, being made of long woolly threads trimmed down to form an embossed and shaped surface. The technique was used to depict parts of a picture such as a bird, an animal or flowers. Glass eyes were often used.

The colouring of earlier Berlin work was soft and natural but with the advent of aniline chemical dyes it became hard and exaggerated; gaudy parrots were perched in over-abundant wreaths of flowers, each depicted with garish luminosity. But eventually colours improved and more interesting tones and pattern combinations were used. Background tones were of crucial importance; there was a great fondness for black from around 1850 but purple, red, green and lighter colours were also used. Birds, cabbage roses and lilies were scattered through every household. Some were inspired by the publication of fine books delineating species; Edward Lear's coloured lithographs of the parrot family, Gould's and Audubon's bird books and the opening of the Zoological Gardens at Regent's Park in 1828 all contributed ideas. With regard to flowers, earlier pieces tended to depict traditional favourites reasonably discreetly, but these were gradually crowded out by larger, brighter blooms, in many cases overblown, blowsy specimens created in hothouses rather than typical of English gardens. They were crushed together in unsubtle colour combinations, a taste perpetuated in some civic gardens today.

Berlin pictures, however, were sometimes of a more substantial form and continued the tradition of imitating great or popular paintings; some of the Bible stories that were embroidered in silk and wool forms were transposed directly to the counted square technique of Berlin woolwork. Well-known masterpieces such as Leonardo da Vinci's *The Last Supper* were enormously popular in various sizes; six versions were exhibited at the Great Exhibition in 1851. Countless identical kits depicting The Flight into Egypt, The Expulsion of Hagar, Moses in the Bulrushes and similar themes were sold and worked without a stitch of originality. Many designs were derived from original paintings, reproduced by the German factories without permission or royalties since no law prevented this till 1842. Paintings by living artists were often 'improved'. Landseer's charming animals were most popular but were unashamedly altered or transposed into different settings. Many patterns were given away with ladies' magazines such as *The Englishwoman's Domestic Magazine*, *The Young Ladies' Journal*, *The Ladies' Treasury* and the *Girls' Own Annual*. These of course were dated. Large and often complex historical subjects provided the greatest challenge and were sometimes worked in relatively small stitches. Finer stitching was sometimes used for faces and other flesh parts amidst thicker sewing, also for details within bolder decorative patterns. Historical and contemporary subjects often showed royal events or members of the Royal Family. A huge picture (6 ft x 5 ft) (1.8 m x 1.5 m) of Mary Queen of Scots is reported to be in a private collection in Long Island, USA. Favourite themes were Mary Queen of Scots mourning over the dying Douglas at the Battle of Langside, and Charles I bidding farewell to his family. Queen Victoria, the young Prince of Wales, wearing tartans, or as a sailor, and the Queen's pets were frequently portrayed, often with charm. An example now at Kensington Palace showing royal dogs, *Islay and Tilco with a Red Macaw and Two Lovebirds*, was after the picture by Sir Edwin Landseer painted in 1839 and placed in the drawing room at Osborne. One needlework version shows the group out of doors with flowering bushes, trees and a castle, all additions to the oil painting. King Charles spaniels and cats sitting on tasselled cushions were often embroidered in pictures, on stools and on cushions.

Baxter prints were another source for needlework, especially views of the royal castles at Windsor, Balmoral and Osborne as well as portraits of members of the Royal Family. They also provided famous, romantic scenes, and a snow scene from the Alps celebrating the new sport of mountain climbing. American Berlin work was similar to English but, in addition to the usual subjects, portraits of George Washington, Benjamin Franklin and topographical designs were embroidered.

In general, after experiments with older forms, Berlin designs were firstly pictorial, then also boldly floral and, lastly, geometrical. The latter two styles were applied to carpets which, being of a large format, were happily suited to the technique. Late-18th-century carpets already

Figure 88
Berlinwork picture of a woman with holly and mistletoe from a pattern supplied with *The Young Ladies' Journal* 1872. (28 in x 20 in).

had formalised patterns, mostly geometric, in shaded colours, and sometimes with optical effects. A revival of leaf designs with a predominance of bright flowers followed and then there were again 'tile' designs made up of squares, roundels and octagons fitted together and often containing flowers or rosettes. The Victorian taste for large blooms in cluttered groups was somewhat restrained by this method of making up carpets of a number of joined squares. Huge examples were made, some consisting of individual panels with complete motifs or vignettes, contrasting backgrounds, differing borders and corner patterns. Screens were similarly made. (*Plate 28a*) All the expected subjects of Berlin work were pieced together in a balanced scrap-book

Figure 89
Victorian banner fire-screen of wool, silk and glass and metal beads the central spray being of fine stitchery.

formation that lacked a great degree of artistry but was none the less effective. Sentimental rural scenes, garlands, birds, animals, children with hoops or kites, real or imaginary butterflies and heraldry provided colourful combinations. A large carpet given to Queen Victoria and shown at the Great Exhitibion was made by 'The Lady Mayoress and 150 ladies of Great Britain' to a design by John Papworth, the architect, and others of squares made by contributors were designed as suitable for presentation purposes.

The Berlin craze might have driven husbands mad since its application seemed endless: 'Two hearth-rugs and an ottoman, seven chairs and after that I hope to do some groups of flowers, and a handsome carriage mat'.[3] It was applicable to many smaller items too, such as blotters, watchpockets, and 'carpet' slippers for the men, as well as for furnishings. The technique could not however be used for garments as it was too heavy.

PATCHWORK AND QUILTING

Second only to Berlin work amongst popular needlework was the making of patchwork coverlets or 'quilts', especially in America, where the terms 'pieced' and 'piecework' are also used. The hobby was barred to none since the materials could be limited to available scraps; however more ambitious attempts were made to collect interesting fabrics and work them into original and elaborate designs. As in the 18th century, fragments cut to various shapes were artistically assembled to make up a unified whole and the best examples were also quilted. Patchwork largely depended on the quality and charm of the fabrics used and the identification of these helps to date quilts. Silks, printed materials and velvets were used independently or together. As the century progressed, the designs tended to be plainer or less orderly; good early coverlets had essentially a Regency feel with geometric effects akin to parquetry or Tonbridge ware. Optical tricks such as the log cabin pattern[4] gave an interesting, lively appearance. American patchwork was especially sophisticated and extensively made as a popular art form; it lacked the dull, commercial sameness of so much of the English needlework of the period. A circulation of patterns was carried out privately and each example was subject to personal variation. The height of American 'quilting' was reached in the first half of the century by which time 'quilting bees', parties at which ladies gathered to do their sewing, were a social institution, and a feature even recorded in song:

Twas from Aunt Dinah's quilting party
I was seeing Nellie home . . .

Some 300 named designs have been recorded, some with loose religious connections such as 'Star of Bethlehem'. Album quilts were also made, usually of squares contributed by individuals, often signed and some-

Plate 28a (top)
An eight-fold screen incorporating one hundred and twelve squares of Berlin-type needlework of great variety, *c*.1850.

Plate 28b (bottom)
A woolwork picture of a lion, *c*.1840.

Figure 90
An unusually sophisticated Irish patchwork quilt of printed fabric, early 19th century. (Centre portion.)

times dated. The pieces were embroidered with a variety of decorative, topical or factual details, and the finished article was often for presentation. Good patchwork was also done in England, Wales and Ireland[5], and some delightful examples have been preserved as heirlooms. A large number of lesser ones of ordinary materials were made for plain practical purposes; even 'a patchwork quilt made from socks' was listed in a recent saleroom catalogue.[6]

Crazy patchwork was deliberately made of irregular pieces, often of bright and deep-coloured fabrics, with embroidered feather stitch joinings (often in yellow) and sometimes superimposed with motifs of embroidery or appliqué. The jagged edges resembled broken pieces of stained glass. Towards the end of the century, kits for making these were available. In America, coverlets of this humbler nature were termed 'slumber throws' and were kept downstairs for an occasional nap.

Felt patchworks made from soldiers' uniforms (*Plate 30*) were often done by men, and frequently included appliqué or embroidered pictures, military motifs, flags, arms or regimental badges. Others were composed of a number of small portraits, scenes or animals around a central subject or device. Embroidered details and captions were added. Three major examples shown at the Great Exhibition were worked by a Scotsman (who allegedly spent eighteen years on his), an Irish policeman and a man from Lancaster.[7]

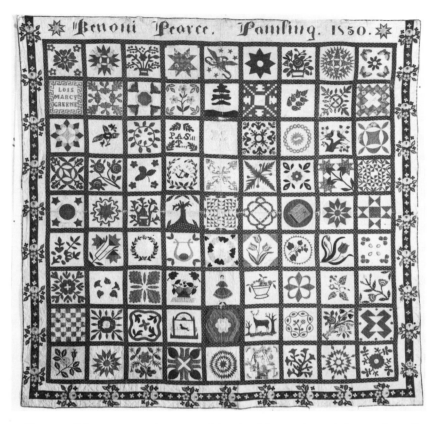

Figure 91
An elaborate patchwork
album quilt, dated 1850.

True quilting was at times combined with patchwork but primarily took a humbler role in the 19th century, being a local, traditional craft in South Wales and the North of England; Scotland was in the meantime largely busy with her whitework industry. Professionals sometimes drew out the designs for quilting in these country areas, and the materials used were inexpensive cottons. Regional examples can be seen in the Welsh Folk Museum, at St Fagan's Castle.

Another country needlework craft was smocking. Strong, natural coloured working garments of linen had complex gatherings of material at back and front, worked in patterns with regional or occupational variations. Distinctions denoting a trade may have made the wearer's skill recognisable at farmers' hirings, but such marks were probably worn partly out of professional pride, like uniforms.[8] By the end of the century a decorative form was adopted into women's and children's costumes, using coloured threads.

AYRSHIRE AND OTHER WHITEWORK

The quick, chain-stitch technique that originated in India and China, and developed into tambour work, was brought to Europe in the 18th century. It was immediately popular and by the middle of the 19th century was practised by half a million workers of white embroidery in Ayrshire and Northern Ireland. The fashion for light, embroidered muslin had grown since the 1790s, especially for children and babies. Known as 'sewed muslin', the fine quality embroidery, so contrary in spirit to Berlin work, was sewn with a hook instead of a needle, in cotton on cotton, and parts had holes filled with semi-lace devices. A French christening robe imported in 1814 greatly influenced the styles developed, and very soon the designs were exclusively of small flowers, decorative filling patterns and light foliage. The embroidery was sometimes done in factories but more often by women at home. R. Samuel, and Thomas Brown of Glasgow in 1857 employed two thousand staff in Glasgow and twenty to thirty thousand outworkers in Scotland and Northern Ireland. A colossal business grew around Glasgow and Paisley but Ireland soon produced strong competition; a large proportion of lower paid women in both countries were efficiently employed by astute organisations on charming and skilled, but repetitive and demanding work. It is indeed well to recall when we admire the delicate 'flowerings' of endless christening robes, frocks and caps, that the 'flowerers', as they were known, were sadly impoverished women who undertook the work to boost their families' meagre wages. The wives of lowly paid miners, smelters and farm labourers, they were given printed patterns with instructions and time limits by co-ordinating agents. At first, each woman worked a complete item but later mass produced single pieces, which were collected for manufacture into garments, laundering and packing at a factory. The women sometimes met in small groups and a child might be paid a small wage to keep up a supply of threaded needles. It was hard labour:

> With fingers weary and worn,
> With eyelids heavy and red,
> A woman sat in unwomanly rags,
> Plying her needle and thread—
> Stitch! stitch! stitch!
> In poverty, hunger, and dirt.[9]

No doubt, working in poor light, the flowerers strained their eyesight terribly; James Morris in *The Art of Ayrshire White Needlework* (1916) reported that women would bathe their aching eyes in whisky to revive them.

Much of the industry was for export to the United States and Europe but some was for sale in Britain. The cotton used was imported, largely from America, and the Civil War there was chiefly the cause of the sudden collapse of the business at the end of the century. But the technique was already being superseded by successful ventures in machine embroidery.

A number of less fine but interesting whitework techniques were

Plate 29
A woolwork, plush and beaded firescreen panel adapted from Landseer's painting of Queen Victoria's pets, with Islay and Tilco below a red macaw and two love birds, and Osborne House in the distance, c.1850.

Figure 92
Elegant Ayrshire embroidery at the foot of a child's long robe, c.1850.

continued, developed or revived, usually from Italian sources, during the century. They were partly associated with lace making and were mostly heavier than Ayrshire work, and for household purposes rather than costume.

Guipure d' Art or *Filet Brodé* was inspired by 16th-century lacis and a return to Vinciolo's pattern book of 1588. It involved darning on hand or machine-made net, imitating the old style. A blunt needle was used to make a variety of stitches to designs advocated in books such as Madame Goubard's *Patterns of Guipure Work* (London 1869). Large items such as bed covers were made up in squares, often alternating with contrasting ones of another type of work, such as broderie Anglaise. This was a coarse cutwork that became fashionable *c.*1825 and developed into a coloured variety known at the end of the century as 'Madeira work', the technique having been most successfully established on that island by nuns from England. Holes in stylised floral patterns were cut out and then edged with buttonhole stitch. 'Richlieu' embroidery also reflected the Italian Renaissance with a heavy lace effect; leaves and flowers were outlined in buttonhole stitch, were joined with bars, and then the rest of

Figure 93
German or Belgian whitework handkerchief with the arms of Queen Sophie of the Netherlands, *c.*1840.

the material was cut away. Coloured materials were again sometimes used. Various *guipure* forms were of similar techniques.

'Coggeshall' embroidery from Essex was a light, white tambour work on muslin and chiefly characterised by designs of wild flowers continuously trailing over the fabric, for costume use.

A number of whitework techniques were fostered in Ireland to encourage employment and utilise cheap labour. 'Carrickmacross' was a simulated lace made throughout the century. Cut-out flower sprigs of thin cambric were applied to net, and infilling patterns were made by drawn-thread stitching. 'Mountmellick' was initiated by Johanna Carter at the village of that name near Waterford in about 1825, and consisted of embroidery in heavy, white cotton on strong, shiny cotton. The designs were again of wild flowers, with oak leaves, blackberries, corns and ferns in textured contrasts of stitching. A quilt of this work dated 1855 is in the National Museum of Ireland. 'Limerick lace', made from the 1830s, was tamboured and then sewn over with infillings of various lace stitches.

Particularly fine and laborious sewing, resembling lace, was done on handkerchiefs. Beautiful examples from continental Europe inspired imitation and variation. A remarkable handkerchief probably made in Belgium around 1840 for Queen Sophie of the Netherlands is now in the Rijksmuseum. On it are eight different drawn-thread background patterns and delicate flowers, a crowned monogram, armorial shields and a scalloped edge in leaf pattern. In America, wedding handkerchiefs called for a focus of painstaking white embroidery.

In 1828, Josué Heilmann of Mulhouse invented a multi-needle embroidering machine that threatened the whitework industry of Scotland and Ireland, but also in some respects encouraged an interest in hand work. The machine could be operated by 'one grown-up person and two assistant children' with up to 140 needles. It was in Switzerland that the techniques were perfected but the English patent rights were bought by Henry Houldsworth of Manchester in 1829; by 1859 his textile firm had twenty machines producing economic trimmings for dresses and table cloths. The patterns were repetitive but accurate and effective, being traced out from a design by the operator with the aid of a pantograph. The products were exhibited at the Great Exhibition in 1851 and at the Dublin Exhibition two years later. Similar machines were used in Switzerland and Germany. Simultaneously, the domestic sewing-machine with a shuttle and continuous thread action was developed by Isaac Singer in New York. By the end of the century, most repetitive work was done by machinery leaving embroideresses free for individual or specialist work. Those employed in the skill still had uniforms, ceremonial and exclusive costumes, and a revival in ecclesiastical needlework to turn to; but many were ready for new inspiration and leadership.

ART NEEDLEWORK, THE ROYAL SCHOOL, WILLIAM MORRIS AND REVIVALS

By the 1870s, there was a strong reaction in England against the absurd dullness and lack of artistry in Berlin woolwork. Branching away from this middle class pursuit, indignant upper class ladies sought more ambitious and interesting projects. Surprisingly quickly they turned to Art Needlework (or Art Embroidery) and this became highly fashionable for a relatively short period of about twenty years. The somewhat self-confident term 'Art Needlework' was applied to a new artistic approach to designs and materials. Obvious pictures and posies worked in garish synthetic colours were dismissed in favour of natural forms relating to drawing and painting. Alongside this a revival of interest in old embroidery, a close examination of it and attempts to repair it led in particular to a revival of crewel embroidery. Seventeenth-century hangings, invariably wrongly referred to as 'Jacobean', were newly admired and these influenced modern leafy patterns which incorporated woodland and wild plants and flowers; larger foliage was often shown as a surround to smaller plants and each subject had a sense of seriousness; 'every flower that sad embroidery wears'[10] was depicted in natural herbal colours. In reaction to the brightness of aniline dyes, these were perhaps made a little too sombre and, due to a determination to use natural dyes, many surviving pieces have faded badly.

Art Needlework was intrinsically English in mood and had a distinctly antiquarian flavour. Natural and garden foliage was blended with a mediaeval historicism, elegance and romance, as cultivated by Sir Edward Burne-Jones and contemporary artists. It also derived aspects from oriental designs and incorporated the development of a Japanese style, as a form in itself. Walter Crane had admired the 'fineness, firmness and precision of workmanship' in Japanese embroidery and the American painter James Whistler decorated his studio with Japanese lacquer and embroidery. Water birds, large leafed plants, sprigs of blossom, clouds and other motifs found their way into all European decorative arts including English embroidery.

Figure 94
Art Needlework hanging 'Autumn', one of three seasons, with blackberries, grasses and other wild flowers, c.1900. (12 ft x 3 ft 9 in).

These new fashions in needlework largely developed in conjunction with the School of Art Needlework, founded in 1872, and later known as the Royal School of Needlework. Under the presidency of Queen Victoria's daughter, Princess Christian of Schleswig-Holstein, its purpose was 'to supply suitable employment for poor gentlefolk' both in the restoration of old needlework and the creation of new. The committee consisted of distinguished and high-minded ladies such as Lady Marion Alford whose book *Needlework as Art* (1886) epitomised the serious approach to the subject. The school employed over a hundred women and undertook commissions, working to designs by leading painters including Burne-Jones, William Morris, Lord Leighton and Walter Crane. Prepared works were supplied for ladies to do in their own homes and the provision of set pieces soon became a substantial business and source of income. An 1880 advertisement[11] for these indicates the practical nature of the pieces chosen for art needlework. Hangings, bedcovers, curtains, screens, tablecloths, cushions, chair back covers, and all sorts of borders were advocated, but the school also listed designs and materials for more curious accessories:

Tennis Aprons, Folding Screens, Kettledrum D'Oyleys,
Photograph Frames, Bellows, Opera Cloaks,
Piano Panels, Babies' Head Flannels, Knitting Pockets.

In fact the craze for art needlework would seem to have almost eclipsed the abundant Berlin work. An amusing cartoon in *Punch* entitled 'Sweet Little Buttercup, or Art Embroidery 1879' depicted a languid female dressed in a garden of embroidery and surrounded by admiring animals in human clothes. In the following year, Elizabeth Glaister described how the new passion for crewelwork made the rooms of many houses look more like laundries, the furniture being draped with embroidered linen. Another lifelong embroideress apparently followed each trend of needlework and had many results to show for it: '. . . she wrought the whole Bible in tapestry, and died in a good old age after having covered three hundred yards of wall . . .'

Other needlework societies were formed, many of them stemming from the Royal School. The Decorative Needlework Society, The Ladies' Work Society and, amongst smaller establishments, the Wemyss Castle School provided constructive employment for gentlewomen. Organisations in Scotland and Ireland stimulated more embroidery. The Donegal Industrial Fund encouraged a type of needlework known as 'Kells Embroidery', the designs being derived from the famous 8th-century manuscript, the Book of Kells, and worked with soft russet and green vegetables dyes, in shades of blue or in whitework.

The Leek Embroidery Society was founded in 1879 by the wife of Thomas Wardle, a textile producer and friend of William Morris. Using his specially dyed silks, the society produced fine embroideries for church use, 'Anglo-Indian' needlework (sewn over imported silks or

printed ones made by Thomas Wardle's business) and a full-scale copy
of the Bayeux Tapestry, now owned by Reading Corporation.

Following the success of the Royal School of Needlework's pavilions
at the Philadelphia Centennial Exhibition in 1876 and at the Paris Inter-
national Exhibition in 1878, a similar institution was instigated in
Philadelphia. This led to further organisations being formed in Boston,
Chicago, New York and other American cities. Teachers were sent out
from London and they naturally propagated styles developed here but
distinct efforts were made to achieve an independent American quality.
In New York, a Society of Decorative Arts was formed by Louis Comfort
Tiffany and Mrs Candace Wheeler to encourage the production and
sale of a wide variety of arts and crafts; related organisations also produced needlework. One project was a set of embroidered gauze bed
hangings made for the actress Lily Langtry's hotel bedroom in London;
another was a striking curtain designed by Tiffany in 1879 for Madison
Square Theatre, depicting a woodland scene with an immense depth of

Figure 95
Victorian four-fold
screen with embroidered
panels designed by
Selwyn Image and worked
by the Royal School of
Art Needlework.

field—a sunny foreground stretching through dense, misty trees to a blue distance. It was worked in appliqué of many materials. 'American Tapestries, made by embroidery alone' were offered by Associated Artists, after early tapestry designs such as Raphael's *Miraculous Draught of Fishes* (Victoria and Albert Museum). In Deerfield, Massachusetts, two New York painters, Margaret Whiting and Ellen Miller, set up an industry in 1896 making blue and white crewelwork, based on simplified 17th-century designs. Flax thread was dyed with indigo and embroidered on linen imported from Russia. Other colours were used latterly. The works were signed with a 'D' within a spinning wheel.

Of the English painters already mentioned, William Morris (1834-96) was the most significant, being directly concerned with the development of needlework. An apprentice in the office of a celebrated architect, G. E. Street, with Philip Webb—another enthusiast, Morris led the cultural reaction following the technical and commercial successes of the Great Exhibition, which had firmly established England in a strong trading position. Dissatisfied with the complacency of the mechanised achievements that served mass production, he resolved to pursue better and more interesting designs linked with a revival of old techniques and craftsmanship. Despising the glibness of machine processes, he turned with fanatical emphasis to hand skills which were superior in some respects but inevitably had limited scope in others. This specialist approach produced many fine works, at best sharing a feeling somewhere between the delicious vulgarity of Mendelssohn's music and the dark richness of Elgar's. But in other respects it led to a short branch line in artistic development, for a major factor was the essentially backward-looking attitude of mediaevalism. Architects and painters sought, with fairy-tale exaggeration, to revive a bygone age.

Morris and the cult which followed his teaching were however extremely thorough in attention to detail; with painstaking enthusiasm they unpicked early pieces of needlework to learn stitches, worked out methods of dyeing and Morris himself embarked on a major project depicting Chaucer's Illustrious Women for his Red House at Bexley Heath, Kent. An eclectic interest in mediaeval facets, such as stained glass and tapestry weaving, were incorporated in his approach to design, contrasting strongly with silk or wool needlepainting of the earlier part of the century. He saw embroidery design as 'midway between that for tapestry and that for carpets' and subsequently it is not surprising that many of his pieces have an oriental flavour. Languid leaves in formal swirling patterns, often flat and feathery, are strictly disciplined, with something of a Persian feeling. Real plants and flowers were advocated but he warned against 'cheap and commonplace naturalism', preferring perhaps a slightly contrived quaintness and naivety. A major contribution of his teaching was an awakening of interest in fine quality materials with rich and glistening colours and textures, intricately worked. No doubt thinking of Berlin work, he pointed out that embroidery 'is not worth doing unless it is very copious or very delicate—or both'. A sense of cultivating beauty was to be remembered: '. . . and also since we are using especially beautiful materials, that we shall make the most of them and not forget that we are gardening with silk and gold thread'.[12] However, Lady Marion Alford objected to the foliate carpet patterns on account of their 'repetition of vegetable forms as being reminiscent of a kitchen garden in a tornado'.

William Morris's firm, Morris, Marshall, Faulkner and Co., was founded in 1861 and announced that it carried out 'Embroidery of all kinds'. This included a considerable amount for church use which was a natural consequence of the prolific church building of the period. The needlework was not particularly ecclesiastical in design but was characterised by tight, intricate patterns of leaves of contrasting sorts, as, for example, in a large wool hanging behind the altar at Lanercost Priory, Cumbria, which was probably designed by Morris and possibly made by his firm. Figures, when incorporated, were largely inspired and sometimes actually designed by Burne-Jones. Vestments were usually of damask, perhaps with additional embroidery; Philip Webb was influential in the design of these. Morris himself designed needlework hangings for his firm, as well as coverlets and other articles for various craftsmen, including Catherine Holiday, the wife of a designer of stained glass and mosaics. She was given a free range of colours and worked in partnership with Morris, discussing with him fine details for things which were to be sold through the business.

The Arts and Crafts Society was founded in 1888 and was a significant sponsor of exhibitions of modern decorative arts, supported by leading artists. Embroidery was one of its chief concerns. Many craftsmen exhibited through the Society including Phoebe Anna Traquair whose fourfold allegorical screen of 1895-1902 in the National Gallery of Scotland is a significant work of the period. Of exceptionally fine quality the panels depict, after an essay by Walter Pater, the four stages in man's spiritual life—the Entrance, the Stress, the Despair and the Victory.

Another screen, of five folds, at the London School of Economics, was designed for the Royal School of Needlework by Walter Crane. The designs are similar in style to his well-known wallpaper *Peacocks and Amorini* and his book illustrations. An elaborate neo-Renaissance type pattern incorporates peacocks, swans and other birds, with monkeys, cupids, fruit and the god Pan. A Greek inscription from Theocritus is quoted at the bottom. (*See* epigram, page 1.)

By the end of the century the Royal School was generally esteemed as a national institution, holding extensive exhibitions and having a wide influence. The starting of a new building for it in 1899 was celebrated as something of a minor state occasion. The Prince of Wales layed the foundation stone, the Life Guards were paraded, the Royal College of Music performed and the Bishop of London offered a prayer before a rendering of The Old Hundredth. But the originality of Art Needlework

Plate 30
A feltwork appliqué hanging with cut-outs of a variety of wild and domestic animals, Daniel in the lion's den and the royal arms above.

was inevitably becoming weakened; reformers started questioning its values suggesting that it was too much an eclectic mixture of 'museum-inspired' styles. There was some truth in this. J. D. Sedding asked for a return to nature and to garden subjects, even suggesting Sutton's seed catalogues as a source for real flowers.

A considerable revival of ecclesiastical needlework, from about 1840, was chiefly led by the prestigious architects of the period, whose ambitions were to restore many aspects of mediaevalism. They built colossal numbers of neo-Gothic churches, hoping to decorate and furnish them in an appropriate vein and reinstate ceremonies with rich vestments.

G. E. Street, with the help of his sister and Agnes Blencowe, founded in 1854 the Ladies' Ecclesiastical Embroidery Society to provide altar cloths based on old examples, or made to modern designs supplied by architects. Amongst these was G. F. Bodley whose drawings were closer to mediaeval origins than many others, in that they were largely pictorial, with figures rather than pattern alone; most designs were not especially religious, being of naturalistic flowers and leaves. Bodley also commissioned work from Morris's firm and from Watts and Co., a business still operating today. There is a banner worked to his design at Peterborough Cathedral. In 1841–2, A. W. Pugin, a prominent architect and partner of Sir Charles Barry in designing the Houses of Parliament, attacked in the *Dublin Review* the 'prettiness' of domestic needlework and urged a return to serious work with 'an appropriate meaning'. He designed vestments for the Roman Catholic Church and preferred a rich background of velvet or cloth of gold. His set of vestments made for St Chad's Cathedral, Birmingham, have a feeling of mediaeval richness with elaborately patterned damask and a liberal use of silver and gold thread. Sir Arthur Blomfield, another prominent architect, also designed embroideries including some for the Radcliffe Infirmary Chapel in Oxford. Street provided designs for Newton, Jones and Willis of Birmingham, a firm that produced catalogues of designs that were popular for church furnishings for many years. But he also saw the potential of amateur embroiderers and spoke of the '. . . happiness which must result from employing their fingers and their eyes upon something fair and beautiful to behold instead of upon horrid and hideous patterns in cross-stitch, for foot stools, slippers, chair-covers, and the like too common objects'.[13]

Several other organisations for church needlework included the Church Extension Association and the School of Mediaeval Embroidery. The serious devotion to this work was epitomised in *Church Embroidery, Ancient and Modern* by Anastasia Dolby, 'Late Embroideress to The Queen' (1867), which was produced more like a Prayer Book or Bible than an instruction manual, being printed in Gothic script and with red lines framing each page.

At the end of the century, a highly secular trend in design, leaning towards 20th-century modernism, became apparent in *Art Nouveau*. Languid and nebulous shapes of a semi-foliate, dreamy nature were adopted in many forms. A considerable stimulus was further fostered in Great Britain through the initiative of the Glasgow School of Art and its Principal, Francis H. Newberry. The emphasis was on simplicity and originality at all costs. Plain embroidery, or applied work, was taught to children in preference to the basic grammar of white sewing, which was said to be bad for the eyes. Materials also had to be simple. Mrs Jessie Newberry and Ann Macbeth advocated the use of the many beautiful fabrics of a cheap kind instead of costly silks or glistening threads. The backward-looking historicity and eclecticism of Morris and his friends vanished into a single-minded, novel clarity. The former may have appeared somewhat unoriginal but the latter was so daringly fresh and so plain that it could not really have lasting qualities except as a curious transitional phenomenon. It was at Glasgow also that Charles Rennie MacKintosh led a distinctive movement that was influential in many parts of Europe, its chief essence being in simple contrasts of curves with vertical and horizontal straight lines.

In addition to the various new trends, well-tried classical forms were continuously executed with little innovation or originality and it can sometimes be difficult to decide whether a thing is of an early date, a legitimate later version, or merely a fairly old pastiche.

Good Chinese embroideries, especially bedspreads, made for the European market, were imported to England until at least 1850, some distinctly 18th century in feeling. These were followed by less beautiful varieties often of dark or garish silks.[14]

NOTES

Epigram: Lord de Tabley, *The Soldier of Fortune*. Quoted by Huish, (op. cit. p. 134).

1 Mallett & Son, 1979. Another very similar sampler of the following year was clearly worked under the same instructress, though the family names are different.

2 Brontë Parsonage Museum, Yorkshire.

3 M. T. Morrall, *A History of Needlemaking*, 1852.

4 The log cabin pattern is made up of bars of material graded in length, and sewn together around a smaller square piece.

5 Irish Patchwork exhibition and catalogue, Kilkenny Design Workshops, 1979.

6 Christies South Kensington, 29th April 1980.

7 There is a curtain of felt patchwork at Bamburgh Castle, Northumberland.

8 One of two fine smocks made for the Great Exhibition (1851) is to be seen at Abingdon Museum, Berkshire.

9 Thomas Hood, *The Story of the Shirt*.

10 J. Milton, *Lycidas*.

11 *Handbook of Embroidery*, 1880.

12 William Morris, *Hints on Pattern Designing*, a lecture in 1881.

13 G. E. Street, lecture to Durham Architectural Society. Printed in *The Ecclesiologist*, vol. XXI 1863.

14 The occasional use of Chinese needlework in association with European furnishings is exemplified by a magnificent Queen Anne bed at Erdigg, near Wrexham, fitted with specially made Chinese embroidery.

7 Modern Needlework

. . . thy mind
Shall be a mansion for all lovely forms.

T HE AMAZING wealth of glorious designs available today is not least amongst the great benefits of living in this age rather than one of those fascinating earlier periods. We have unlimited access to the resources of the world and the experience and techniques generated through past centuries. The richness of the heritage from which we can so readily seek counsel and inspiration, with the availability of both natural and man-made materials should enable us to create some of the finest achievements of all time. But the trends of the 20th century have unfortunately not yet produced needlework of that excellence. Although it is still too early to judge, it would at present appear that since the end of the 19th century, needlework, like most other art forms, has been desperately feeling for a course and experimenting inconsistently in an effort to discover a satisfactory identity. A number of satellite fashions have shone with varying qualities, a few with distinction, but a general theme and direction has not yet been established. The Embroiderers' Guild, an educational charity, founded in 1906 to promote the craft to the highest possible standards, has been influential in co-ordinating new ideas of design and technique. The Guild also has a substantial historic collection which has recently been moved to the organisation's new headquarters at Hampton Court Palace.

The art of needlework from mediaeval times progressed in multiple ways, identified and co-ordinated by a unity of purpose and feeling which disciplined and contributed to skills and designs. The relatively recent lack of integration originated only in the last century when no permanent form emerged after a series of revivals. William Morris was the principal pioneer of the modern movement but failed narrowly to achieve a style descendant from the wide scope of historical and cultural forms which had influenced him. He was perhaps too retrospective in his approach, neglecting the philosophy of contemporary technical achievements, and unable to accept the benefits they had to offer.

Machinery superseded many domestic crafts but did not threaten needlework since its products replaced only what had already become artless. Some forms of mass-produced embroidery were still carried out by hand, as at Arthur H. Lee and Sons, of Birkenhead, Cheshire, where decorative crewelwork curtains were made to old designs, with coarse

Figure 97
Oxford v. Cambridge
Boat Race on the Thames
embroidered in wool,
*c.*1920.

wools and using up to four threads in the needle at once. These and other traditional designs were carried on timelessly as long as fashion demanded. Crewelwork made in India for the European market is still available by the yard in London department stores.

More ambitious attempts at originality with a wide range of materials were tried out simultaneously. Ann Macbeth's designs were distinctly simplified, light and consciously not overworked. She enjoyed considerable success supplying designs to Liberty's and other shops. Elaborate stitching was not much favoured until after the influence of Cubist painters in the 1920s, when texture was again considered important. Three-dimensional effects reminiscent of stumpwork, but much less intricate, were attempted and quick appliqué became fashionable again, often on a huge scale.[1] Vestments designed by Matisse for the chapel at Vence are of applied work in a strong, bright design. The technique is a very ancient and effective one but often the quality of workmanship is limited. The celebrated Overlord Embroidery,[2] commemorating aspects of the Second World War and made by the Royal School of Needlework is of appliqué and on a massive scale, being 272 feet (83 metres) long and reminiscent of the mediaeval saga hangings, besides its obvious parallel with the Bayeux Tapestry. Its artistry is in reflecting the illustrative techniques of the period such as newspaper photography; it does this remarkably, and very much with the favoured colours and textures of the times. The subject depicted is suitably momentous and eminently worthy of such a large-scale work.

A less serious but charming hanging, of three panels, totalling about 28 ft in length, was designed by Belinda, Lady Montagu to mark, in 1979, the 900th anniversary of the New Forest. It combines, in a rich variety of textures, appliqué work, canvas work and embroidery, and depicts vignettes of historical and social interest within a general theme of natural history.[3]

Figure 98
Section of the massive
Overlord Embroidery
depicting H.M. King
George VI, General
Eisenhower, Field
Marshal Montgomery,
Field Marshal Alan
Brooke and Sir Winston
Churchill.

A number of embroideresses have been prominent in attempting to stimulate fine needlework: The Hon. Mrs Rachel Kay-Shuttleworth (*d.*1967) was a collector and teacher founding a centre for study at her home, Gawthorpe Hall, Lancashire; Mrs Theodore Roosevelt Jr. (*d.*1960), daughter-in-law of the American president, was another notable and versatile embroideress. Her pictorial designs for screens and pictures contain an element of humour; one picture portrays a 'Sea Serpent' while a screen depicts monkeys swinging about in tropical vegetation. The tradition of patchwork quilting has also been carried on throughout the 20th century in America and in England, where it has taken more the form of a revival.

In canvas embroidery, however, the emphasis has been on novel designs and interesting stitches, a prominent contribution of needlework teachers. A large amount of work has been directed to kneeling hassocks and cushions for churches; many cathedrals have impressive quantities of neat and bright needlework, standing out against a foil of stone and woodwork in majestic settings. Some of the work is rich in design and intricate in workmanship. Good examples can be seen at Lichfield, St Albans, Wells and Exeter cathedrals. At Winchester, a body of about 200 embroiderers was co-ordinated by Louisa Pesel on a project known as 'A St Swithin's Day Enterprise', making kneelers and cushions. Miss Pesel had previously done needlework for the private chapel of the Bishop of Winchester at Wolvesey, based on 17th-century sampler designs. Artistically and technically she adhered to two fundamental rules that are crucial to successful embroidery. If the work is to be multi-coloured, the variety of stitches must be reasonably limited and conversely, if a variety of stitches is to be displayed, a limited range of colours should be used. In monochrome embroidery a variety of stitches gives shading and textural interest.[4] This was especially a feature of blackwork and early crewelwork.

Figure 99
The 14th-century stalls at
Wells Cathedral are
decorated with fine
woollen cushions and
hanging panels, c.1937.

Plate 31
A fine modern design
based on an 18th-century
form, and incorporating
wonderful movement,
colours and shading.

Nowadays 'serious' modern needlework is made with high pretensions, usually in picture form, or as hangings, often to be regarded as 'fine art'. Divorced from utilitarian characteristics, it is often gross in scale and design and like so much of the 'art' of our times, aims to shock our sensibilities. Some pieces show bold strokes of originality, sometimes in an exciting way but often wild, confused and undisciplined, with little true content.

Beryl Dean however has been responsible for some remarkable pieces which combine a feeling of the times with interesting technical innovations and, above all, appropriateness. Her cope, stole, mitre and morse made for the Bishop of London on the occasion of the Queen's Silver Jubilee in 1977, echo in a collage effect of specific architectural motifs, a sense of binding unity which is embodied in Church and State. The design includes St Paul's Cathedral, seventy-three London churches

Figure 100
One of five panels by
Beryl Dean representing
scenes in the life of the
Blessed Virgin Mary,
this one showing the
Visitation, 1973.
(8 ft x 4 ft 8 in).

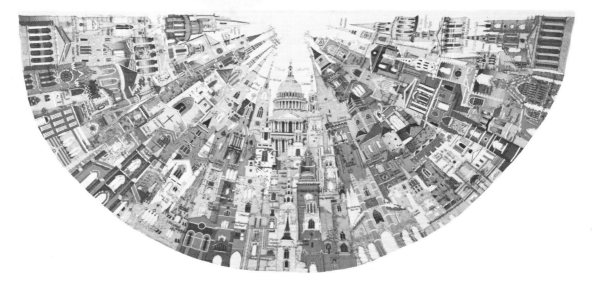

and two Royal Peculiars. Some modern vestments attempt to draw our
attention by the use of brilliant colouring but these Jubilee pieces are
especially attractive being worked in subtle and harmonious shades of
yellow-golds and silver-greys.

Colour judgement is one of the most important factors of needlework
and one of the least understood. The softness, subtlety and brilliance of
good dyes are perhaps more crucial even than a good design. Dr Johnson
quoted a useful extract from Addison in his *Dictionary*:

> In a curious brede of needlework, one colour falls away by such
> just degrees, and another rises so insensibly, that we see the
> variety without being able to distinguish the total vanishing of the
> one from the first appearance of the other.

This may have been referring to Florentine embroidery but the sugges-
tion of blending tones is a general lesson for all needlework.

The catchword 'soulless' is sadly as applicable to much modern
needlework as to other aspects of contemporary arts and crafts but it is
to be hoped that the position will be rectified by a humbler re-examina-
tion of the invaluable and inestimably beautiful work bequeathed by
previous generations. A willingness to recognise continuity and to
derive an essence from the best is the crux of creating works that will
uplift and adorn the age. We have an important responsibility to con-
tribute to the world's artistic achievements; the resources at our finger-
tips are tremendous; we can travel almost anywhere to consult wonderful
designs and can see countless ideas through photographs and books.
A new style, neither brutal nor twee, would help to restore self-confidence
and interest; perhaps 'post-modernism' will provide it. There are,
happily, signs in architecture, and elsewhere, of a strong new form, with

a definite language of historical learning, coupled with a richer depth of
metaphor. Bald functionalism has had its day and, unashamedly, the
age-old grammars are at last being used and extended as the basis of
exciting new achievements. Surely the very richness of historical
needlework ensures that the future of the craft will be continuously
buoyant?

NOTES

Epigram: W. Wordsworth, *Lines composed a few miles above Tintern Abbey*.

1 Cf. the Egyptian appliqué hangings of the 1920s, many brought to England.
2 To be seen at the Overlord Gallery, Whitbreads Brewery, Chiswell Street, London,
  EC1.
3 New Forest District Council, Lyndhurst, Hampshire.
4 Further good examples of needlework cushions and hassocks can be seen at Girton
  College, Cambridge and in many churches. At the Community of the Resurrection,
  Mirfield there is a 'tapestry' derived from a mediaeval manuscript.

A Note on Costume

N ELABORATE display of costume has been used in many periods as a symbol of status and power; a great show of it was intended both to instil fear in subordinates and to secure the confidence of supporters. At political and social levels an outward appearance of wealth expressed sway, but an element of personal vanity was blended with this. In the late 16th century Sir John Harrington unashamedly admitted: 'We goe brave in apparell that wee may be taken for better men than we bee; we use much bumbastings and quiltings to seem fitter formed, better shouldered, smaller waisted, fuller thyght than we are. . . .'

The French mediaeval courts were especially sumptuous with magnificent costume. Even the Duchess of Burgundy's fool had an embroidered costume made for him in 1421 with emblems and pearls on it. Charles d'Orléans had music embroidered on his costume, the notation indicated by 500 seed pearls.

Italian costume was not generally rich in needlework since that country specialised in and preferred to wear fine, woven fabrics. In England, however, the Tudor court was splendid with most elaborately embroidered dress. Princess Mary Tudor, daughter of Henry VII and later wife of Louis XII, had her footmen dressed in white cloth of gold quilted with a scale pattern. Henry VIII's costumes were renowned for their lavishness and some, like many others of the period, are faithfully depicted in paintings. They are seen to be heavily laden with gold thread, precious stones and pearls. (*Plate 9*)

Elizabethan dress was even more remarkable and was painstakingly portrayed. Many aspects of it have already been mentioned but a further example of the intricate detailing, a description of ruffs by Philip Stubbes, of 1583, may be added. He speaks of them as: '. . . either clogged with gold, silver, or silk lace of stately price, wrought all over with nedle woorke, speckled and sparkled heer & there with the sunne, the moone, the starres, and many other antiquities straunge to beholde'.

Mary Queen of Scots' wardrobe was carefully listed, together with substantial records of her needlework on garments. Especially significant was a skirt which she made with great pains for presentation to Elizabeth I: '. . . a skirt of crimson satin, worked with silver, very fine and all worked with her own hand, to the Queen of England, to whom the present was very agreable, for she found it very nice and has prized it much'. Mary Queen of Scots had spent three months working on it.

Dress materials and embroideries were greatly treasured and were unpicked and re-used in various forms until completely perished. For this reason few have survived to the present day. Sometimes costumes were adapted for use as coverings for furniture. An item in Henry Howard, Earl of Northampton's inventory of 1614, includes embroidered slips and borders cut from a cloak 'to imbroder some furniture for the howse withall'.

In Charles I's reign a greater availability of fine silk fabrics caused less embroidery to be used for costume. Plainer garments displaying the lustre and colours of the silks were favoured but a man's dress would include ornamental lace collars, cuffs and an embroidered scarf. The last item was originally worn over one shoulder and tied below the opposite arm, and later around the waist. A fine purple scarf worn by Charles I at the battle of Edgehill is in the Victoria and Albert Museum. A descendant of this form of garment is still worn by soldiers in the army today. Another scarf is at the Nottingham Museum of Costume, where many other early items, including those of Lord Middleton's splendid collection, are to be seen.

Eighteenth-century dress was highly decorative and pretty needlework was liberally used with a less formalised, flowing elegance. Mrs Delany, in 1738, described both the men's and ladies' costumes worn at the Prince of Wales' birthday party. The Countess of Huntingdon had a petticoat of black velvet covered with embroidered vases of flowers, shells and foliage. On other occasions petticoats were decorated with crewelwork of amateur workmanship, and of similar designs to bed curtains. As referred to earlier, the Boston Gazette in 1749 cited an American example, that had been stolen. It was worked with 'Deer, Sheep, Houses, Forrest, etc.'

Crewelwork costumes were less formal than the fine silk embroidery worn by older and grander ladies. Much needlework on dress was professional work, especially the more sophisticated patterns and varieties with metal threads, the heavier ones being known as bullion. Bugles, spangles, coils, aiglets and beads were used in quantities but were soon snipped off when, with the fashionable craze of 'drizzling' or 'parfilage', every girl robbed old embroidery ruthlessly to sell metals for re-use. Even Prince Leopold boasted earning enough by it to buy a silver soup tureen, which he gave to Princess Victoria on her eleventh birthday.[1]

The embroidering of clothes was a general pastime attempted by all and was not debarred from high-born ladies; even Queen Charlotte and her daughters enjoyed doing needlework on their dresses, including silver thread work. Metals of contrasting patterns and textures were displayed especially on the extraordinary 'mantua' dresses which became fashionable. These protruded sideways from the wearer's hips,

Figure 103
Red silk mantua, heavily
embroidered with silver
bullion, *c.*1745.

supported horizontally by paniers (hoops), and, with matching trains and shoes, were usually of professionally made embroidery.

Huge quantities of metal thread, braids and tassels were used for military uniforms in the 18th century and onwards; the weight of the materials contributed to a stiff smartness, the essence of correct turnout. The emblems depicted on grenadier caps and other such accessories called for a high standard of professional needlework.

A gentleman's domestic costume in the second half of the 18th century could be very bright and flamboyant. Waistcoats and frock coats were of a wide variety of beautiful fabrics, often ornately embroidered with floral or sometimes more unlikely designs. A French waistcoat of about 1780 in the Musée Historique des Tissus, Lyons, is decorated with monkeys, flower sprigs and sprays, symmetrically placed on both sides.[2] Other equally flippant designs were displayed on the portly figures of 18th-century gentlemen.

Regency fashions were similar though less florid, with a tendency towards plainer patterns and the use of limited combinations of colours. But with the introduction of Berlin wool embroidery the range of new opportunities for canvas work led to a mass of ephemera, such as the countless slippers made by admiring ladies for their suitors, together with waistcoats and smoking caps.

Much less fashionable, but more interesting in retrospect, are the

165

Figure 104
Part of an unusual set of
appliqué panels of
contemporary dress
materials, perhaps
representing the marriage
procession of George III,
c.1785.

peasant smocks that were made in English rural areas for use by agricultural and other workers. Of Anglo-Saxon origin, these garments were of plain, homespun linen or twill material, with regional variations of style and colour, ranging from olive green in the Fens to black in Surrey and the Isle of Wight. A few were worked in two colours but most were of a natural off-white. Sussex smocks were the most elaborate. Central panels of 'tubing' on the back and front, surrounded by a 'box' of embroidery and pulled together pleats of material provided a strong area on either side of the garment. Differences in design could signify the trade or skill of the wearer and the embroidery might include indicative devices such as a shepherd's crook or sheep.

A folk costume with town associations is that worn by the Pearlie Kings of costermongering in London. Now an established tradition, though only begun in this century, these are elaborately decorated with mother-of-pearl buttons.[3]

The fashionable dresses of recent *haute couture* have had to be dazzling and sparkling. The designs of Norman Hartnell and Christian Dior for ladies of the Royal Family have been characterised by interesting collages of texture and soft-coloured reflective sparkles intended to stand out with appropriate individuality. They also provide a foil for fine jewels.

NOTES

1 *Country Life*, February 6th, 1953. Sylvia Groves, 'The Practice of Parfilage'.
2 The design is in the Cooper-Hewitt Museum.
3 Margaret Lambert and Enid Marx, *English Popular and Traditional Art*, 1946, p. 34.

Plate 32
An early-18th-century
walnut wing chair
upholstered with
contemporary needlework
c.1720.

A Note on Heraldry

NCIENT AND colourful heraldry and the art of needlework have been closely allied since the Middle Ages; the two were combined for practical purposes rather than solely decorative ones and the execution was magnificent. Heraldry was an essential language of society, a means of identification, and embroidery provided the chief method of depicting it. In wartime battles and peacetime tournaments horses, riders and banners carried clearly and boldly the distinguishing blazon of noblemen and gentry. The display of their arms was as large and impressive as possible to emphasize the power of the bearer; medieaval documents show how spectacular such occasions were. The designs were usually of appliqué in bright, basic colours with much use of the metals, gold and silver. Smaller pieces were often of raised (padded) work, and the majority were produced in workshops by professional men.

The great seals of mediaeval monarchs, such as those of Edward I, II and III, show their chargers clad in fine heraldic trappings; effigies on tombs depict a wealth of heraldic embroidery, always of a formal or official nature but also magnificently decorative. The identification of heraldry today is a complex science but even a slight reading knowledge greatly increases an appreciation and understanding of many historical artefacts, including needlework.

Reference has already been made to the Black Prince's jupon of quilted embroidery with the royal arms on velvet, which was suspended over his tomb in Canterbury Cathedral. This is a rare and fascinating relic. The old and modern heralds' tabards, as for example the series in the Victoria and Albert Museum that belonged to two generations of the Anstis family, both Garter Kings of Arms, have similarities of form being heavily embroidered with a clear display of the royal arms on back, front and sides for instant recognition.

Mediaeval banners, from which modern flags are derived, were strictly heraldic and were carried in battle and flown on tents and castles. They were symbols of their bearers' presence or of allegiance, a recognisable mark of authority, and used in the same way as the Royal Standard and Arms are today. The length of mediaeval banners was gauged according to rank. The king's standard was eight to nine yards long, a duke's was seven, an earl's was six, a baron's was five, a baronet's

Figure 105
Large firescreen panel,
c. 1745, with the arms of
Home impaling Western,
against a dark olive-
green background.

was four and a half and a knight's was four yards long. Pennants, badges, shields and streamers all glittered at tournaments especially, but battle-fields were colourful too. Beauchamp, Earl of Warwick, under Henry VI, took to France with his army 'sixteen standards of worsted entailed with the bear and a chain' which was his heraldic symbol. He also took a colossal streamer, forty yards long and eight yards wide, similarly embroidered with heraldic creatures. Other banners bearing religious symbols in heraldic fashion were taken to battle representing the Trinity, Our Lady, St George and other saints. Henry V took several such banners to Agincourt as well as ones with his arms.

Heraldry was also prominent in non-military circumstances, even in combination with the highly religious iconography of ecclesiastical vestments. The early-14th-century Syon cope (Victoria and Albert Museum) has a complete border of arms in lozenges and roundels. Two hundred years later heraldic emblems were frequent in church needle-work and especially on funeral palls. An early-16th-century one in Cambridge is of Florentine, black, cut velvet on a gold ground, with the royal arms of Henry VII and a crowned Tudor rose and crowned port-cullis embroidered in silk and gold threads on linen, applied to cross bands of wine-coloured velvet.

City livery companies and parish churches had fine palls, often with heraldic needlework. The Pewterers' Company has a pall dated 1662 of cloth of gold with its arms on it. The Company also had a banner made with its arms for use at pageants.

Heraldic embroidery of an official type is represented by such items as the charter bags of Edward I's and Edward II's reigns preserved at Westminster Abbey and also in the possession of the City of London.

Figure 106
Detail from a procession of the Knights of the Garter, *c.*1530.

Figure 107
Chester Herald wearing a
tabard of velvet richly
embroidered with the
sovereign's arms.

The former is of green cloth, with a red shield embroidered with the
arms of England, 'three lions passant gardant, or'. The royal arms were
always displayed on throne canopies and usually in raised form. Two
interesting survivals of 1617 and 1660 are preserved in the Museum of
Antiquities, Edinburgh.

Heraldic devices were also embroidered in a less formal, more
decorative manner on costume and furnishings. Illustrations of Richard
II at the time of his deposition show him dressed in black, powdered
with ostrich feathers, and his horse trappings and pennon bore the same
badge. Similarly, furniture was decorated with individual insignia,
impressas and emblems of varying degrees of heraldry or metaphor.
The Black Prince bequeathed in 1376, 'our bed of camora [camel hair and
silk] powdered with blue eagles'. His widow bequeathed in 1385, 'my
new bed of red velvet embroidered with ostrich feathers of silver and
heads of leopards of gold with boughs and leaves issuing out of their
mouths'.

In the Tudor period heraldry took on an important decorative role,
but also maintained full political and social significance. Chairs of state
and beds proudly displayed their occupants' insignia. Henry VIII had
a bed with: 'the Kinges Armes holden upp withe great Anteloppes
upon the Testor . . . the said Testor beinge . . . fringed on bothe sides
with a narrowe fringe of Venyce golde read and purple silke and lyned
with red bokeram . . .' The royal arms, crests and monogram insignia
continued to be embroidered (professionally) on beds, especially
valances, well into the 18th century. They were also, of course, prominent
on symbols of high office: a portrait, dated 1579, of Sir Nicholas Bacon,
Lord Keeper of the Great Seal of England, shows him with an embroidered bag which contained the seal. Other officials of State had similar
bags, burses, or purses, magnificently embroidered with the royal arms.
Lord Eldon, who held high office for a long period, 1799–1827, had so
many that his wife had them made into bed hangings.[1]

From the late 16th century heraldic shields became a principal motif
in embroidered cushions, table carpets and similar household furnishings.
Mary Hulton's cushion and the Gifford table carpet, both in the Victoria
and Albert Museum, depict arms prominently and charmingly. Armorial
cushions continued to be popular for a long time, partly in imitation of,
or as alternatives to, Dutch tapestry ones. They provided a formal
though decorative display of status and were worked in wools in long
and short stitches more often than tent-stitch on canvas.

The orders of chivalry called for needlework. An early garter, of the
Order of the Garter, is at Anglesey Abbey, where other heraldic embroidery is also to be seen. A mantle of the Order of the Thistle, in a
private collection, was worn by the Earl of Perth when the order was
revived by James II in 1687. It is of green velvet embroidered with gold
thistles and with a shoulder badge depicting St Andrew. In 1703 Queen
Anne re-formed the order, instituting a plain green velvet mantle.

Figure 108
A variety of whitework
stitches suggest heraldic
tints on this linen pillow
sham. Perhaps Swiss,
*c.*1850.

A large amount of elaborate regimental needlework was carried out
from the 17th century; examples may be seen in the Army Museum and
other collections.[2] A Purse of the Honourable Artillery Company
dated 1693, of red silk decorated with arms, trophies and the initials
'W M' is in the British Museum.

Crowned and plain monograms were often embroidered on household
furnishings, hangings, book covers and boxes. An example in gold
appliqué of *c.*1680 is to be seen on a walnut settee at Holyroodhouse,
Edinburgh.[3]

From the early 18th century, heraldry was increasingly depicted in

picture form on carpets, on banners and screens, especially small pole screens. A successive tradition of similar work continued throughout the 19th century up to the present day. The designs were often provided by professionals. In 1738 'David Mason, Japanner' advertised his services, offering 'Coats of Arms, Drawings on Sattin or Canvis for Embroidering'. In New England, memorial hatchments were made in needlework, a practice not attempted in Great Britain. Several examples may be seen at Winterthur Museum, Delaware.

Domestic heraldic embroidery has more recently included the arms, crests or badges of institutions, colleges and regiments, worked as pictures, chair seats, cushions and kneelers for churches. Modern varieties of these, together with more ambitious heraldic projects, call for skill and accuracy without great artistic demands, but they are timelessly appropriate, effective and very decorative.

NOTES

1 *Country Life*, Jan. 29 & Feb. 5, 1981. Judith Banister 'Rewards of High Office'.

2 Regimental colours, trumpet and kettle-drum banners display splendid, professional heraldic needlework. The styling has changed very little over two hundred years.

3 *The Dictionary of English Furniture*, Ralph Edwards, 1954, 'Settees', fig. 6.

4 Tent-stitch heraldic needlework for seat furniture is well represented by a fine set of twelve drop-in seats on sofas and stools at Squerryes Court, Kent.

Figure 110
The Royal Arms, an Edwardian banner firescreen.

A Note on Furniture

INUTELY DETAILED illuminations in mediaeval manuscripts often show rich canopies, bed and wall hangings.
The fact that they were prominently portrayed indicates
how highly they were valued. These textiles were undoubtedly treasured as were ecclesiastical vestments; the
latter were stored flat in great chests, such as the magnificent half-round
one for copes at Gloucester Cathedral. But few secular materials have
survived and details have to be gleaned from inventories. Fragments of
information such as the fact that Edward VI's gown of 'black velvet
embroidered very richly' was later used on a footstool, help to make up
an historical picture.

The word 'furniture', until recently, was used more generally to
include all decorative and useful 'movables', but in many early records
the term was used specifically to refer to bed curtains. These were
amongst the most valuable items of a house and are often listed at the
beginning of an inventory next to the cloths of estate or throne canopies.
Elaborate state beds were of symbolic importance in a house as well as
the focal point of official and social activities, even birth and death. They
were thus lavishly furnished with hangings fitted by an upholsterer (or
French *tapissier*), considered the most important craftsman until the
full emergence of woodwork in the 18th century, when carving, gilding
and painting became important. Fine beds displayed status and wealth
and, never at risk of being regarded ostentatious or vulgar, many were
of costly needlework. Heavy metal threads, silks and velvets were used
on the most important. Crewel embroidery on others was less expensive
and more durable, so as a result more of these have survived. They were
often worked by their owners. Lady Anne Drury of Hardwicke, Suffolk,
for example, bequeathed in 1621 'a cloth bed of my own making'. Beds
became less important towards the end of the 18th century when
bedrooms were considered private places and were smaller and less
prominent in the architecture of the house. American and British patchwork quilts and other coverlets however continued the fascination in
bed furnishings into the 19th century and modern times.

The magnificence of early beds is clearly indicated in wills, and the
descriptions are almost poetic: 'one large bed of black satin embroidered
with white lions and gold roses and escutcheons of the arms of Mortimer

and Ulster'. This reference of 1380 recalls the heraldic creatures so often featured in hangings. An item in a will of 1434 records the colourfulness of late mediaeval textiles: 'my bed of silk, black and red, embroidered with woodbined flowers of silver, and all the costers[1] and apparel that belongeth thereto. . . .'

A century later Mary Queen of Scots returned to her kingdom to find the royal residences rough and bare. She immediately brought from France embroiderers and *tapissiers* and had many beds erected for herself, her attendants and her fool. Some were embroidered, others were of appliqué and trimmed with silk braids and some were of warm wool with worsted fringing. Wool linings were essential as insulation against the cold and damp. Mary's excellent chamberlain, Servais de Condé, recorded many interesting details and we know for example that of twenty sets of hangings and canopies of estate brought to Scotland in 1561, twelve were embroidered, some with the ciphers of her French relations and some with 'histories', that is, narrative illustrations of stories. One bed was described as having 'six pands (i.e. valances) roof, headpiece and three underpands' showing the labours of Hercules.

Figure 111
Queen Anne needlework for the top of a folding walnut card table with *trompe l'oeil* playing cards, counters and a pocket watch, on a green background.

This was probably the bed inherited by James I and recorded at Hampton Court in 1659. Tent-shaped beds were also listed at this period and field-beds, still elaborate but more easily packed and moved. In 1562 Mary Queen of Scots confiscated a number of possessions from the rebel Earl of Huntly including yellow damask bed hangings 'made like a chapel' and altered into a four-poster. She also took many vestments which the Earl had in safe keeping for Aberdeen Cathedral and had no qualms about adapting these to secular use. Some were given to Bothwell and 'a cope, chasuble and four tunicles to make a bed for the King (i.e. Lord Darnley). All broken and cut in her own presence'. A green velvet set was used for a bed, a high chair, two seats and a *chaise percée*.

Large numbers of needlework cushions were an important feature of the furnishing of a room and many were listed of various materials. An inventory made at Edinburgh Castle in 1578 lists ten chairs and as many as forty cushions. Two stools 'coverit with sewit werk of divers culloris' are in the same inventory but chairs and stools were far less numerous than soft furnishings, and were reserved for the most important visitors or the chief members of the family. Like beds they were invariably covered with luxurious fabrics. In 1543 Princess Mary gave her father Henry VIII a chair which cost about £4, but the needlework covering for it cost no less than £18. A splendid painting at Sherborne Castle depicts Queen Elizabeth I going in procession to Blackfriars. She is being carried in a litter, the canopy of which is embroidered with flower slips, clearly depicted in what was probably a larger format than the actual sewing. Meanwhile James I's horse-drawn carriage, now in the Kremlin, is upholstered with a needlework interior.

An increase in comforts in the 17th century called for further hangings and upholstery. Curtains were not used for windows until the 18th century but 'coverlets' were sometimes hung over windows and doors. The Hardwick Hall inventory of 1601 lists 'a coverlett to hang before a dore' and 'thre coverlets to hang before a windowe'. These may have been of tapestry or needlework. Bed hangings, however, continued to be made with great laboriousness and cost. The Countess of Salisbury had a set made professionally in time for the birth of her daughter in 1612. They were of white satin embroidered with silver and pearls, and were said to have cost a fortune. James II ordered a bed, two armchairs and six stools to be made in Paris by Simon Delobel at a cost of £1,515. The uses of needlework became greatly extended as it was made for considerable quantities of furniture in addition to beds and wall hangings. Canvas embroidery was much more durable than crewelwork for upholstery, but the same design in both techniques is occasionally seen together on complementary furniture. In other cases designs are clearly related: a wing chair and five other armchairs at Boughton House are covered with needlework of a red leaf-design reminiscent of crewelwork. (A similar pattern in greens or blues is sometimes seen in other canvas embroidery.) Florentine needlework was used on walls and on beds as

Figure 112
Early 18th-century
French chairback, the
central semi-oriental
panel worked in tent
stitch and the surrounding
pattern in coarser cross
stitch.

well as for covering seat furniture. Another set of chairs and stools at
Boughton illustrate this.

By the end of the 17th century a wide range of decorative items were
either wholly embroidered, or incorporated pieces of needlework. In
Antwerp pictures were made for use in the doors and drawer fronts of
cabinets; this technique was similarly carried out from time to time in
England.[2] An interesting mahogany cabinet, *c.*1745, recently acquired by
Temple Newsam in Leeds, incorporates floral panels of tent-stitch
with chenille on the outside and twenty-two small silkwork drawer
fronts on the inside.

Pictorial subjects became increasingly popular, based on classical, allegorical stories or fables, and sometimes in the form of Dutch still-life flower groups. Such themes formed the basis of needlework seat covers for single chairs or sets of furniture. A scene was often portrayed in a reserve, worked in fine tent-stitch, and a surrounding border of flowers was worked in coarser stitches. Many good pieces of this format have survived; examples can be seen at Waddesdon Manor, Scone Palace, Seaton Delaval, Northumberland and in the Frick Collection, New York. English and French tent-stitch work were similar; the latter is sometimes distinguished by a tendency to have the design against a white background, and to depict more exotic plants, especially pomegranates.

Two pairs of large Régence armchairs and a sofa in the Frick Collection are covered with very good tent stitch work in excellent condition, even if of a somewhat later date, as suggested of some of it. One pair is especially delightful, having a light blue background decorated with polychrome motifs including Venus, cupids and small mythological landscapes amongst animals, masks, shells, ferns, flowers, swags, scrolls and lambrequins, reminiscent of Berain.

English wing chairs of the first half of the 18th century were particularly favoured as a vehicle for elaborate canvas embroidery and many good examples have survived. The designs ranged from pictorial forms to general or specially arranged floral patterns. Queen Anne and George I chairs were especially fine; there are two magnificent ones in the Untermeyer collection at the Metropolitan Museum and two others at Clandon Park. Fine needlework on squarer, Chippendale period wing chairs, is rare but a pair from Hornby Castle, embroidered by members of the Godolphin-Osborne family, are notable. They are variously decorated with flowers in sprays and growing up a trellis, with a cream background. A pair of sofas was also embroidered in the same manner.[3]

Many ambitious projects were undertaken. The Great Parlour Chamber at Weston Hall, as already mentioned, has an impressive quantity of needlework made by Mrs Jennens c. 1731, while at Nunwick, Northumberland, including a bed and six chairs; there is a set of furniture by Lady Allgood c.1750, consisting of a settee, six chairs, stools, card tables and firescreens. A portrait of the embroideress shows her holding an embroidered seat. She is reputed to have had a spinning wheel fitted in her coach.

Chair backs and seats were frequently, even usually, made first and then an appropriate chair was ordered for them. The Duke of Atholl ordered from William Gordon a famous set of eight mahogany armchairs for Blair Castle, with carved scales on the legs, for needlework which had been worked by the Duchess. Gordon's bill for these is dated 1756.

Professionally made needlework chair seats and backs are represented by a set on ten giltwood fauteuils at Scone Palace. Depicting mediaeval, mythological and oriental scenes in yellow reserves surroun-

Figure 113
A pair of mid-18th-century chairs with unusual original needlework depicting domestic animals on the backs.

ded by a red foliate pattern, these were probably supplied by the *tapissier* Planqué at St Cyr. The chairs were made by Pierre Bara in 1756.

Ornate needlework usually looks best on chairs of a simple line but Chippendale, whose furniture designs of 1754 are generally noted for considerable rococo flourish, recommended tapestry coverings 'or other sort of Needlework' for chairs in the French style. Though it was not the case in England, on the European continent needlework was usually regarded as the poor relation of tapestry and for less formal circumstances.

Chair coverings of plainer forms, and in a limited range of colours were also made. These often imitated or echoed damask with bold formal leaf patterns in red, blue or green. Examples of this kind at the Bowes Museum[4] and at Temple Newsam, Leeds, where there is also an extensive set of gilt furniture consisting of twenty chairs, four sofas and a day bed upholstered in bold and colourful mid-18th century floral work in tent-stitch and French knots.

A remarkable set of mid-18th-century English mahogany chairs with very fine needlework covers has recently been sold in the USA.[5] There are twelve side chairs, two armchairs and a sofa (plus a stool, when previously sold) all with floral needlework. The designs are repeated on pairs of chairs, with alternating colours for the backgrounds to the flowers and surrounding formalised borders.

Simpler designs were increasingly preferred from about 1770. The tidiness of tambour embroidery on silk suited elegant French furniture; this was also used for large screens. Good examples of tambour work and other needlework are to be seen at the Musée Nissim de Camondo, Waddesdon Manor and the Metropolitan Museum, where there are two pairs of chairs by George Jacob, *c.*1775, upholstered with tambour embroidery in the style of the textile designer Philippe de la Salle.

Table carpets, fire screens and other items also offered endless opportunities for displaying needlework and from the first many unexpected or smaller items were decorated with embroidery. Two early-18th-century objects at Parham Park, are representative. The first is a Queen Anne baby's or doll's cot which has a quilted coverlet and upholstery of cream satin. The second is a banner firescreen of delicate and brilliant workmanship; like contemporary pictures it depicts a shepherd and shepherdess on hillocky ground, with a dog, a sheep, a house and trees, within a floral border.

A large number of panels were made for Georgian firescreens and many fine examples have survived. A twofold Chippendale mahogany screen, sold by Sotheby's, contains for example a pair of chinoiserie panels with Chinamen wearing exotic pagoda hats.[6] Pole screens were more usual. An interesting one at Robert Adam's Osterley Park, designed in 1777 for the Etruscan room, contains a relatively rare example of true neo-classical needlework,[7] which is different from the large number of sentimental classical ladies depicted on shield-shaped and oval screens.

Some 19th-century needlework lent itself well to complementing furniture. Berlin wools were used for fairly traditional floral coverings and for chairs, even large sets, as at Burghley House, while new formalised Berlin-type patterns added to the richness that the Victorians sought; bright colours and complex designs contributed to a density of atmosphere and the best of it was certainly impressive. The work was undemanding technically and as it was done with strong materials much has

Figure 114
An 18th-century sofa covered in about 1840 with needlework in shades of green, pink and cream.

survived. *Prie-dieu* chairs and hanging fire screen banners offer a wide variety of designs, techniques and materials. A round conversation sofa at Wallington Hall and curtains at the Bowes Museum, with bold relief flowers, especially roses and lillies in plush stich, represent the delights of fully-flown Victoriana. Couched chenille silks are combined with Berlin woolwork on curtains at House of Dun, near Montrose. Art needlework was not suited to upholstery, the designs and workmanship being too random and fragile, but it was none the less favoured for large screens and wall hangings as already described. Table cloths, furniture runners, curtains, *portières,* piano covers and bell-pulls were amongst the many other articles on which it could be shown.

A large amount of needlework has been done in recent years for covering furniture, usually antique or favourite pieces. Most of it is inevitably of a traditional form appropriate to the age of the furniture. Its success always depends on the quality of the design and the dyes of the threads. Unfortunately, good patterns are difficult to obtain. Lady Victoria Wemyss has worked an impressive number of seats and backs of a charming design for mahogany dining room chairs, with blue and white porcelain and pergolas depicted against a rich red background. This was inspired by a chair formerly at Hardwick Hall and now at Chatsworth, Derbyshire. A hanging of a similar design has recently been seen in the London art market. Designs supplied by most retailers are deplorable; and it is sad that many hours are wasted on charmless, expensive kits. The only satisfactory solution is to create, adapt or copy a good design, consulting any source whatsoever, from printing to pottery, have it transferred correctly to canvas, and seek out wools or silks for it of especially good quality, and magically beautiful dyes. It is in doing this that the art lies, the rest is merely operational.

NOTES

1 'costers' were wall hangings.

2 A Flemish ebony and tortoiseshell cabinet, inset with needlework panels appeared for example in a sale at Christie's, 11th December 1980.

3 See Christie's catalogues Thursday, March 27, 1958 (lot 101) and Thursday, June 30, 1977 (lot 31A) for details and references.

4 Eight chairs and a sofa from Faulkbourne Hall, Essex, with a red floral pattern on a blue background.

5 Sotheby Parke Bernet, Apr. 25, 1981 (lot 71). *See also The Connoisseur*, March 1964, J. F. Hayward, 'An English Suite of Furniture with embroidered covers'.

6 *The Connoisseur* February, 1980. Gillian Walkling, 'Jack of all Work, Screens from East and West'.

7 Ibid.

A Note on Collecting

Reculer pour mieux sauter

ORMING A collection of needlework may be done on several levels; making a general survey, making a specialist study, or gathering a few pieces within a wider collection. If any of these are taken seriously, in each case the essence of success is in concentrating on 'the best', and in striving for quality rather than quantity.

An occasional glance at the astonishing bulk of needlework produced over many years can be made by visits to mixed accumulations in the sale-rooms, and an acquaintanceship with many different items is valuable. A true collector, however, will want to limit himself to special examples only and will be determinedly blinkered in the pursuit of quality, picking out only articles of unusual interest and beauty. If passionate, he will be prepared to, and will learn to 'up-grade' his pieces in a continual process when the opportunity arises, adding finer examples and disposing of all but the best. Of course good collections are shaped also by personal character, allowing for a sentimental element, and incidental aspects which may be technically contrary to the guiding principle; certainly items with exceptional charm or of a special interest deserve a place as they can add a dimension. This is particularly the privilege of a private collector as opposed to a museum.

Building a collection or improving one is in itself an art; arranging it can be another. In both, the crux of the matter is certainly selection; a serious collection or study depends on an ability to discard the majority of what one sees in order to allow time and energy for an intensive consideration of a relatively small number of pieces. That is half the art of collecting. The other half is a matter of developing 'an eye' that recognizes what is exceptional over and above sheer quality—an ability to feel for things which possess special genius or charm, overriding the technical considerations. It is not necessarily only the pieces of finest quality that constitute a good collection, and the creative activity of sifting deciding factors is all part of the art and fun of collecting.

The opportunities for private collectors are still considerable so the enjoyment to be derived from perpetually culling and seeking is immense. Whatever knowledge and expertise one has, or however experienced, the finding of a remarkable piece is always exhilarating. Moreover one is never too old to discover surprises of technique,

Figure 115
An 18th-century seat with
a charming variety of
flowers and foliage,
c.1740.

Figure 116
Small Louis XV bead-
work book-binding, of
coloured and white
beads. French *c*.1750.
(4¾ in x 3¾ in).

style or design, and as needlework is uniquely individual, and seldom recorded, there are no limits to the possibilities of variation. Though many of the most important survivals of early needlework are now in museums and other permanent collections, good and interesting items appear on the market sporadically. In addition to generally accepted touchstones, many curious and beautiful pieces of all periods provide opportunities for serious consideration. The prices now paid for some important pictures and hangings might appear to be prohibitive but needlework is still generally undervalued in relation to the other decorative arts. It is right that the most celebrated items should be in public collections; the richness of these pieces provides a reference for the large number of collectors and students outside their walls. But many essentially domestic products are periodically available to be newly acquired and enjoyed by true enthusiasts and, once the needlework bug has taken hold, there is no remedy for the 'incurable collector'.

Glossary

ACUPICTURA Needlepainting; embroidery representing subject in as accurate detail as possible and resembling painting, or imitating it.

ALBUM QUILT Patchwork, usually American, made up of a number of sections contributed by various individuals, each designed by the sewer and sometimes signed. Often for presentation.

APPLIED WORK, APPLIQUÉ Cut-out pieces of fabric laid and stitched onto another in patchwork form. An ancient and continuously popular technique.

ARABESQUE Low-relief decoration in form of scrolls, interlacing strapwork, curving lines, sometimes with animal and leaf motifs. Of oriental and Moorish origin, especially introduced through carpets.

ASSISI EMBROIDERY Needlework that originated in Assisi in north Italy characterised by formal designs, the motifs left unworked against a background entirely filled in with cross-stitch.

BARGELLO *See* Florentine stitch.

BAROQUE Exuberant, florid style of the second half of the 17th century, sometimes heavily ornate, always lively; aspect of late-Renaissance florid flourish in contrast to earlier strict, academic classicism. Associated with lavish use of metal thread work and with bold crewelwork designs.

BEETLE WINGS Used as sequins for luminosity, in ethnic, American and English costume embroidery.

BLACKWORK (SPANISH WORK) Monochrome embroidery, usually in black, sometimes enriched with metal threads, fashionable in 16th century, and brought to Europe through Spain by the Moors.

BLANKET STITCH Similar to buttonhole stitch (q.v.) but with the loops spaced out; often used for edging as on wool blankets.

BROCADE Woven textile with a raised pattern, with metal threads, silks etc.

BRODERIE ANGLAISE Mid-19th century cutwork, white embroidery characterised by oval and round holes in light cotton fabric, closely edged with stitching, and with some additional padded satin stitch embroidery. A coloured version adopted in Madeira.

BURATO Whitework darning on gauze or net. Compare with net laces, filet or lacis (q.v.).

BURSE Ecclesiastical: stiff, square pocket to contain linen cloth (corporal) used at Holy Communion; also formal bag, as carried by the Lord Chancellor for example, often elaborately embroidered, in which a seal is carried.

BUTTONHOLE STITCH Simple loop-stitch, one of the oldest and most popular, especially suited for edgings, but its chain form has been applied to all forms of embroidery.

CALICO   Cotton cloth, originally from Calicut on the west coast of India.

CAMBRIC   Linen material, originally from Cambrai in Flanders; also more generally applied to cotton, or cotton and linen fabric.

CANVAS   Strong, unbleached cloth of hemp or flax, as sailcloth, for tents and for painting on. Open mesh variety of wool, linen, hemp, cotton or jute used for needlework. Berlin canvas was of a silk covered weave as the background was left unworked. A canvas of double threads was introduced in 1830's (*see* Penelope), though multiple threads had been used in the 17th century.

CHAIN-STITCH   The chief of many linked, loop stitches. Ancient and universal, it has been used for outlines and infilling, and is done either with a needle or hook ('ari' in India, 'tambour' in France). Quickly made, it is frequently the only stitch used in sizeable hangings; in small workmanship lends itself to shading. Also made by early sewing machines.

CHASUBLE   Vestment worn by priest officiating at the Eucharist; a large, almost circular garment, in the middle ages often magnificently embroidered. In the 16th century the shape altered to a long round-ended vestment, leaving the arms free of the heavy material.

CHENILLE   Soft, fluffy thread, usually silk, though also of cotton or wool, with furry appearance like a caterpillar (French *chenille* = caterpillar). Used from about 1770, chiefly for small contrasting areas in conjunction with plainer canvas and embroidery stitching.

CHINOISERIE   European imitation of Chinese decoration in lacquer, needlework etc., often recognizable by caricatured features.

CLOTH OF GOLD   Rich fabric, generally of silk, with gold threads woven into it.

COIF (QUOIF)   Close-fitting cap worn by men and women from the middle ages to the early 17th century, latterly finely embroidered; worn on semi-formal and domestic occasions.

COLIFICHET   Floss silk embroidery on paper.

COPE   Ecclesiastical cloak worn by dignitaries on festal occasions, a large semicircular garment often of rich materials or fine embroidery. *See also* pluvial.

CORNUCOPIA   Horn of plenty. Motif showing a curved horn filled with an abundance of flowers, fruit, etc.

COUCHING   Technique whereby a thread is laid over fabric and attached to it by an additional one sewn over it. Technique especially used for metal threads. *See also or nué*, underside couching.

COUNTED THREAD STITCHES   As opposed to freehand embroidery stitches, these are regular ones based on a build-up of simple stitches over an equal number of threads in canvas or fabric.

CREWEL (CRUL, CRUEL, CREWELS ETC.) -WORK, -WOOL   Strong, two-ply, lightly twisted, worsted yarn of home manufacture, extensively used for domestic embroidery of hangings, furnishings and costume since the Norman Conquest.

CROSS-STITCH (*gros point*)   Simple and ancient double stitch in the form of an X, used in almost every part of the world.

CUTWORK (*opus scissum*) Fore-runner of needlepoint laces in 16th and 17th centuries and extensively revived in the 19th century. Parts of white fabric are cut away and then infilled by patterns of crossed threads, with elaborate variations.

DALMATIC Ecclesiastical vestment worn by deacon at Eucharist, normally a short tunic. An historic garment also worn by the sovereign at coronation ceremony and by a bishop, under his chasuble.

DAMASK Fabric of silk originally, but also of linen etc., with woven design in same colour. Originally associated with Damascus.

DARNED EMBROIDERY Simple oversewing, popular especially in the 18th century for silk pictures of birds, fruit, flowers etc.

DARNING SAMPLER Sampler specifically exercising varieties of darning methods and patterns; popular in England in the late 18th century, perhaps introduced from Holland.

DIMITY Stout cotton fabric, usually having a stripe pattern in the weave, used undyed for hangings.

DOSSAL Curtain, or hanging, placed behind altar or around chancel, sometimes embroidered.

DOUBLE RUNNING- (HOLBEIN) STITCH The chief stitch of blackwork (represented in Holbein drawings) whereby lines of embroidery are made up by measured stitches in one direction and completed by infilling stitches in the return. *See* running-stitch.

DRAWN-THREAD WORK Needlework that forms patterns by pulling threads of fabric aside or out, the resulting holes forming design.

DRESDEN EMBROIDERY (*point de Saxe*) Fine, drawn-thread work on muslin as less expensive alternative to lace in the 18th century.

ERMINE STITCH A detached stitch for speckling background, consisting of a long stitch superimposed with a cross-stitch, often in metal thread, on velvet, silk or satin.

EYELET STITCHES Small stitches worked outwards from a central point, forming little rings. Often seen forming lettering in samplers.

FEATHER STITCH A coral or fern-like stitch, composed of blanket stitches forming zig-zag links along a line. *See also* long-and-short stitch for a different variety of the same name.

FLORENTINE (HUNGARIAN, BARGELLO, FLAME) STITCH Work in wavy, zig-zag design on canvas in shaded colours. Forms effective pattern for wall hangings, bed curtains and upholstery. Originated in Hungary in the late middle ages, and later practised in Italy and most of Europe. Modern varieties equally timeless and effective.

FLOSS SILK Soft, untwisted silk of fine strands from the outer part of a silkworm's cocoon.

FRENCH KNOT Knot-like stitch usually used in close formation for flower centres, depicting sheep etc. Chinese Pekin knots are similar.

FUSTIAN Thick, cotton twill, sometimes with linen warp, woven like velvet with a sheared surface. Name derived from Fostat, suburb of Cairo.

GALON Trimming braid used for uniforms, upholstery etc., of silk, wool or metal threads, or of lace.

GOBELIN STITCH   An almost vertical stitch which in rows gives the semblance of woven tapestry.

GOLD THREAD   Is made of finely beaten out gold, wrapped around silk thread. Pure gold was used in the early middle ages but later silver-gilt replaced it, the expanding silver carrying a sufficient coating of gold to a greater extent. An alternative was the use of fine gold leaf laid on thin animal tissue.

GROS POINT   Cross-stitch (q.v.). Loosely used as term for coarser canvas work.

GUIPURE D'ART   Darned net. *See* lacis.

HASSOCK   Church kneeler, especially favoured object for modern needlework.

HOLBEIN STITCH   *See* double running-stitch.

HUNGARIAN STITCH   *See* Florentine stitch.

KNOTTING   Craft carried out with a shuttle, producing knotted threads of string, linen or other materials, then laid and couched on a ground fabric in border form, or in patterns. Practised in the late 17th and early 18th centuries for hangings, chair coverings, etc.

LACIS   Handmade netting darned with patterns, with coarse lace-like appearance, but very ancient in itself, and often highly complex. Designs often in squares, of a stylised nature, following pattern books. Also known as filet, *guipure d'art*, etc.

LAIDWORK   Long threads, sometimes floss silk, laid on fabric and fixed at points by couching threads, at regular or irregular intervals. *See* couching, underside couching.

LAWN   Fine, light-weight, white fabric, originally linen, more recently cotton, used for baby clothes, handkerchiefs, bishops' sleeves, etc.

LINEN   Age-old type of cloth of exceptional comfort and durability made of flax fibres.

LONG-AND-SHORT-STITCH   Old and continuously used simple stitch used in silks and wools. The outer row is of alternately longer and shorter stitches, but rows built within this, in brick fashion, are of equal sized stitches. Also known as feather stitch (*opus plumarium*), etc.

LONG-ARMED CROSS-STITCH   Cross-stitch where the first of the two stitches is twice the length of the second. Hence a series of stitches gives a woven effect.

MANIPLE   *En suite* with a stole, a shorter strip of material, sometimes embroidered, worn by a priest over his left forearm at the Eucharist. A symbol of the towel used by Christ at the washing of the feet of His disciples.

MANTLE   Cloak, sometimes ceremonial. Heraldic mantling, like foliage, around a coat of arms represents a mantle shredded through gallantry in battle. Also, the richly decorated cover placed over the Scroll in Jewish ceremonies.

NACRE WORK   Embroidery with small pieces of mother-of-pearl.

OPUS TEUTONICUM   Mediaeval German whitework, in contrast to the bejewelled and colourful embroidery of other countries, especially England.

OR NUÉ   Shaded gold embroidery. Technique whereby gold threads are laid horizontally, couched-down with coloured silk threads at densely close intervals where dark shades are required, and sparsely for lighter areas, forming shading in a pictorial design.

ORPHREY   Band, usually of embroidery, superimposed in cross or 'Y' formation, or as border, on chasuble, cope, etc.

PAISLEY PATTERN   Takes its name from Paisley in Scotland where imitations of Indian fabrics were made in the 19th century. The characteristic motif of a tapering and curved lob is anciently derived from a buta, a pine cone, mango or kind of plant.

PANE (S)   Joined widths of material in strips as for hangings, or in making up a counterpane. Also the formal slashes in 16th-century costume, allowing under-fabric to be seen.

PANED   Striped, as in certain hangings.

PEKIN KNOT   Like French knot (q.v.), but more loop-like in appearance.

PENELOPE CANVAS   Canvas of threads woven in parallel pairs invented in 1830s and named after the wife of Ulysses who spent nights unpicking work done during the day, in the absence of her husband.

PETIT POINT   Tent-stitch (q.v.). Usually applied to finer work only.

PIQUÉ   Embroidery where the design is outlined with cord and infilled with stitches resembling a figured fabric.

PINKING   Decoration of material by cutting, or punching holes or pattern in it, to reveal under material, or along edges to prevent fraying.

PLUSH-STITCH   Loop-stitch, taking its name from plush fabric, which has a long nap in excess of that of velvet. Loops may be left or trimmed to various degrees to give sculptural effect.

PLUVIAL   Ceremonial cloak or cope (q.v.).

PORTIÈRE   Curtain or hanging to cover a door, sometimes of needlework.

POUNCE   Method of transferring design, (and the powder used), whereby pattern is 'pricked' out and charcoal dust, or another kind, is rubbed through the perforations onto fabric, to mark it.

PURL   17th-century metal thread embroidery, and the thread itself.

RATIONAL (PECTORAL)   Metal or embroidered panel worn by bishop at church ceremonies, derived from Jewish High Priest's breastplate.

ROCOCO STITCH   Groups of about three or four straight stitches tied together by a binding stitch across the middle producing the effect of small holes between each group.

RUNNING-STITCH   Simple continuous linear weaving in and out of fabric at regular intervals. *See* double running-stitch.

SAMITE   Prized mediaeval fabric, thought to have been a heavy silk.

SARCENET   A fine, light silk fabric, first made by the Saracens.

SATIN   Twill-weave fabric of silk or other materials made glossy by being calendered (passed through heavy rollers), which process could also produce a moiré, or watered appearance.

SATIN-STITCH   Straight, parallel stitch, a mass of them giving flat, shiny, satin appearance.

SCRIM   Fine, openweave, brown linen canvas, much of it imported from Russia.

SERICULTURE   Silk farming.

SLIP   Motif derived from a gardener's cutting; a sprig with flowers, buds or fruit with a few leaves and often a heel for planting. Used as a spot motif (q.v.).

SPANGLE   Small glittering object of various materials, usually metal, attached to embroidery for sparkling effect.

SPLIT-STITCH   Very fine stitch worked in untwisted silk thread where each stitch pierces the thread giving a tiny, fine, chain-stitch appearance. Used for delicate detailing, as of facial features in *opus anglicanum*.

SPOT MOTIF   Individual motif such as floral slip (q.v.), animal, insect, etc., usually on linen or canvas, to be cut out, often for applying to another material.

STEM-STITCH   Outline stitch where continuous back stitches each partly overlap in following the line.

STOLE   Long narrow band, often of needlework, worn by priests at Eucharist.

STRAPWORK   Type of decoration in form of interlacing curved and angular bands in regular patterns, derived from Moorish and oriental sources. *See* arabesque.

TABARD   Herald's garment blazoned with the sovereign's arms.

TABBY   Watered fabric, especially silk, brindled, streaked—as cat.

TABBY WEAVE   Plain over and under weave.

TAFFETA   Thin silk cloth, sometimes now of other materials, even man-made.

TENT-STITCH   Plain, diagonal stitch across one thread of canvas or other material. May be worked in horizontal rows or diagonally, usually the former.

TESTER   Originally the part of a large, canopied bed at the head end, reaching from the pillows to the roof; later the canopy itself, whether suspended over the bed or supported by four posts, also sometimes listed as the 'celour'.

TICKING   Closely woven, twill fabric of linen or cotton, chiefly used for containing down in pillows, and hair in mattresses. For the former it is soaped on the inside.

TRAM   Weft (q.v.). Also preparatory laid-thread on canvas to pad out stitches and to cover rawness of canvas where it might show between stitches.

TRAPUNTO   Form of quilting where a soft padding is inserted through the under material, after the quilting stitches have been done, to emphasise a relief design. In Italian quilting a cord is inserted in the same way between parallel lines of stitching.

TROMPE L'OEIL   Pictorial deception making the spectator think he is looking at the actual subject depicted, rather than a representation. Playing cards, counters, etc. are sometimes embroidered on the lining of card tables, for example.

TURKEY WORK   Post-mediaeval wool knotting in carpet form, in imitation of imported oriental ones, used for upholstering furniture etc.

TWILL   Fabric in which weft threads pass over one warp thread and under two or more, producing diagonal lines in the weave.

UNDERSIDE COUCHING   Mediaeval method of attaching laid metal threads whereby no couching threads are visible on surface or prone to wear. The securing threads are stitched over the metal one and then pulled back to the underside of the fabric holding a loop of metal thread.

WARP AND WEFT   The interlaced threads in weaving, the former fastened lengthwise in the loom and the latter woven at right angles through them.

WHITEWORK   General term applied to needlework of white threads on white or natural ground; Ayrshire embroidery, etc.

WORSTED   Yarn of sheep's wool, where long-stapled fibres are combed parallel and closely twisted.

ZEPHYR MERINO WOOL   Berlin wool, firstly produced in Gotha, Germany, and dyed in Berlin for woolwork; popular in the 19th century. Later also made in England.

Figure 117
An Elizabethan cushion cover with red and pink rose sprigs within blue and green strapwork on a yellow ground, perhaps made for sedilia in a church.

Bibliography

READING GOOD descriptions of old textiles can be nearly as enjoyable for a reasonably experienced enthusiast as seeing them. I am particularly grateful for the following books which are highly recommended.

Beck, Thomasina *Embroidered Gardens*, London, 1979.

Bridgeman, Harriet, and Elizabeth Drury, (Ed.), *Needlework: an illustrated history*, London, 1978.

Clabburn, Pamela, *The Needleworker's Dictionary*, London, 1976.

Edwards, Joan, *Crewel Embroidery in England*, London, 1973.

Hughes, Therle, *English Domestic Needlework 1660–1860*, London, n.d.

Huish, Marcus B. *Samplers and Tapestry Embroideries,* London, 1900.

Kendrick, A. F., *English Needlework*, 2nd edition revised by Patricia Wardle, London, 1967.

Morris, Barbara, *Victorian Embroidery*, London, 1962.

Sebba, Anne, *Samplers; Five Centuries of a Gentle Craft*, London, 1979.

Swain, Margaret, *The Needlework of Mary Queen of Scots*, London, 1973.

Wingfield Digby, G. F., *Elizabethan Embroidery*, London, 1963.

Comprehensive bibliographies are included in the second and third of the above titles. A selected list for further reference is as follows:

Catalogue of the Morris Collection, William Morris Gallery, Walthamstow, 1969.

Illustrated Catalogue of the Loan Exhibition of English Decorative Art at Lansdowne House, February, 1929.

Trésors des Musées du Kremlin, Catalogue of exhibition, Paris, 1979.

Victoria and Albert Museum, London, 1928, Picture Books: *English Embroideries; Part I, Elizabethan, Part II, Stuart.*

Victoria and Albert Museum, London, *Notes on Applied Work and Patchwork*, 1959, and *Notes on Quilting*, 1960.

Alford, Lady Marion, *Needlework as Art*, London, 1886, Republished 1975.

Ashton, Leigh, Samplers, *Selected and Described*, London, 1970.

Baker, Muriel, *Stumpwork: The Art of Raised Embroidery*, New York and London, 1978.

Bath, Virginia Churchill, *Needlework in America*, New York, 1979.

Carbonell, Dorothy, *Winchester Cathedral Embroideries*, Winchester, 1975.

Photographic Acknowledgements

COLOUR PLATES

Bath Museum of Costume   Plate 10a
Birmingham Museums and Art Gallery   23b
The Duke of Buccleuch and Queensberry   2, 11a
Christie's, South Kensington   19
Colchester Museum   28a
The Cooper-Bridgman Library   5
Francis Egerton/Peter Maitland   31
Jan Kot   3b, 4, 15a, 15b, 16a, 16b, 16c, 20c, 25c, 27b
Kunsthistorisches Museum, Vienna   8a
Mallett & Son   1, 3a, 10b, 13a, 13b, 14a, 14b, 18a, 18b, 20a, 20b, 22, 23a, 24a,
    24b, 25a, 25b, 27a, 28b, 30, 32
The National Trust   12, 21a, 21b
Parham Park Collection, West Sussex   11b
Reproduced by gracious permission of H.M. The Queen   26
Sotheby's, Belgravia   17, 29
Victoria and Albert Museum, London   6, 7, 8b
Walker Art Gallery, Liverpool   9

BLACK AND WHITE FIGURES

Ashmolean Museum   Figure 50
Clive Bartlett   2, 15, 19, 74, 99, 105
Burrell Collection, Glasgow Art Gallery   41
Hubert Chesshyre   107
Christie's, South Kensington   28, 95
Cogenhoe Church   117
Cooper-Bridgeman Library   1, 4, 14, 18, 20, 21, 24, 25, 35, 36, 44, 78, 91, 93,
    103
Cooper-Hewitt Museum, The Smithsonian Institution   33
Durham Cathedral   11
Beryl Dean/Millar & Harris   100, 101
Audrey Field   92
Christopher Gibbs Ltd   39
Cora Ginsberg   37, 38, 62
James II Galleries   97
Jeremy Ltd/Jan Kot   5a, 5b
Kilkenny Design Workshops   90
Jan Kot   46, 47a, 47b, 48, 55, 60, 61, 75, 79, 80a, 80b, 84, 87, 88, 89, 94, 102,
    111, 116
Leicester Museum   77
Mallett & Son   7, 9, page xxii, 40, 42, 45, 49, 51, 52, 53, 54, 56, 58, 59, 63,
    64, 65, 66, 67, 68, 69, 70, 72, 73, 82, 85, 86, 96, 108, 109, 110, 113, 114, 115

197

Index

Numbers in *italic* refer to the colour plates.